GLEANINGS FROM A WILD GARDEN

GLEANINGS FROM A WILD GARDEN

Excerpts, Essays, and Works in Progress

by John Hanson Mitchell

SCRATCH FLAT PRESS

ALSO BY JOHN HANSON MITCHELL

*The Garden at the End of Time: Getting
by in the Age of Climate Change*

Legends of the Common Stream

*An Eden of Sorts: The Natural
History of My Feral Garden*

*The Paradise of all These Parts: A
Natural History of Boston*

The Rose Café: Love and War in Corsica

Looking for Mr. Gilbert

Following the Sun: A Bicycle Pilgrimage

*The Wildest Place on Earth: Italian Gardens
and the Invention of Wilderness*

Trespassing: An Inquiry into Private Property

*Walking towards Walden: A
Pilgrimage in Search of Place*

Living at the End of Time

A Field Guide to Your Own Backyard

*Ceremonial Time: Fifteen Thousand
Years on One Square Mile*

ISBN: 979-8-9948960-0-6
Library of Congress Control Number: 2026912617

Contents

Preface

Back in June of 1973 I was in the Azores, sitting in a café on Faial, when I got an idea for a book. At the time, I was looking across the straights at Mount Pico, the highest point in Portugal and I thought I would arrange to climb the mountain to get a view of the so-called Triangle Islands and the wild seas and the sky beyond. The Azores lie in the mid North Atlantic far from the busy, warring clamors of the continents of the Western World, and it seemed a good spot to gain some perspective on current events.

The book would not really be about my ascent of Mount Pico however, it would be an extended essay on the current state of the environment and how the recently evolved Cro-Magnon mammoth hunters had come to the point at which they (or we, in fact) were able to invent a bomb that would, in a matter of days or weeks, destroy the world as we know it.

This, by the way, was the decade in which the doomsday clock of The Union of Concerned Scientists stood at two minutes to midnight. Anti-nuclear rallies were taking place throughout Europe and the United States. Furthermore, there was an unpleasant American war going on in Vietnam that I was attempting to avoid, and I had recently joined a huge anti-war demonstration in

Trafalgar Square, one of the largest protests I had ever attended.

In this same period, new industrial assaults on the natural world were stirring up more street protests as well as legal challenges to polluting industries and destructive new developments, including the controversial construction of the Glen Canyon Dam, across the Colorado River. In other words, the time seemed right for a grand overview of how we came to this pass.

I never did write that book. But what I did do was spend the next forty years writing books and essays on the same subject.

This book is a collection of those works in the form of essays, diaries, journal entries, excerpts from published books, as well as works in progress, all of which in one way or another deal with my continuing interest in the interrelationship between nature and human cultures.

This is not some grandiose academic tome; it's a personal exploration of past and present events which I managed, I hope, to contain by focusing most of the books on a single square mile of agricultural land in eastern Massachusetts known as Scratch Flat.

The first book in the series, *Ceremonial Time*, set the stage. It is a fifteen-thousand-year history of the square mile that begins with the retreat of the glacier and ends somewhere in an unknowable future.

Subsequent books, as well as a series of essays from magazines and editorials carry the theme onward. Some of the excerpts are taken from various works in progress, including a book about Henry Thoreau and Robin Hood and the fight to preserve the commons, and a memoir (of sorts) of the years I lived in Paris in the midst of the Algerian War.

Readers may encounter some repetitions in this collection, but that might be expected since I've been hammering out the same theme for forty years. All told, I think I have managed to cover everything I planned to do, and then some, in my ambitious ascent of Pico.

PART ONE:
ENCOUNTERS

Where It All Began

Setting: I'm having a drink in the public square in the small town of L'Île-Rousse on the north coast of Corsica where I have a job at a local restaurant and pension. My Polish friend Magda, the equivalent of an older sister, joins me. She's from Warsaw and has seen the worst of the Nazi atrocities towards Jews and is now a professor at the London School of Economics and married to a sculptor who was a student of Henry Moore. They're spending a month at the pension.

The following week, while I was having a drink in the plaza, I saw Maggs coming out from the little temple-like market stalls across the square.

When she arrived at my side of the plaza I called out to her, and she joined me at the table.

"What are you doing here?" she asked.

"I'm hiding from Vincenzo," I said. "There is a mess of fish back there to clean, potatoes to peel, onions to chop." She ordered a demi of beer and we watched the action on the square. The boule players were forming a new game.

"They come here every afternoon," I told her. "The same old men."

"This must be their way of ordering their world," she said. "People now do not have that so much anymore, the old ways."

She sipped her beer and looked at them again.

From the first time I saw her, Maggs had reminded me of someone I thought I knew, but watching her here, out of context, I realized that she looked like the American actress Eva Marie Saint - high cheekbones, winsome blue eyes, blond hair.

With the lines formed, the small man called Henri took up his boule and made the first cast. It was a modestly good throw, and there arose among the assembled a dull chorus of approval.

Another made his pitch, a wide shot that generated no comment.

And then another. And then a fourth.

Maggs looked back at me.

"They do this every day, don't they?"

"Heavy rain keeps them in," I said. "But not wind."

Just then a one-armed man took up his post. The mumbling of the chorus softened. He scraped away a few stones with his left foot. Stood eyeing the cochonnet, bowed, tipped his arm, and threw. The boule swept over the pitch, angled down, and nestled against the little pig. A kiss. A palpable kiss.

"That's Robespierre," I told Maggs. "He's the best of the lot here."

"Robespierre is his name?"

"Yes, the barber told me that. He was a leader of the resistance network around here. Lost his arm in an ambush on an armored car. Robespierre was his code name. They all had code names. That little man with the squinty eyes was known as Mouse, but they don't call him that anymore."

"What do you do?" she asked. "Come down here all the time and watch? How do you know all this?"

I told her that on certain days I would come here in the late afternoon, take a drink, and watch the action on the square, but on other days I would go out to the Ile de la Pietra to the tower, and at other times I would hitch a ride and take a hike in the maquis, alone.

"What a life," she said.

"Yes, but I also have to clean fish every day and get pricked by rascasse spines." I showed her my swollen thumb.

"You know, it's odd," she said. "I saw you sitting here, and I felt a flash of something, maybe it was just recognition but maybe something else. You look more natural here. I see you more as you are, perhaps. You do know that we're on to your trick, don't you? You play at being that dimwitted busboy who shuffles out from the kitchen in his stained apron and sweeps the floors or cleans fish and pretends not to know what's going on. But I see you listening. I see you pretending not to understand French or even English when you want. Speaking in Italian with Vincenzo. You are more than they all think you are, aren't you?"

"Well, cleaning fish was never my ambition, exactly—I don't think."

"What is?" she asked bluntly.

This stopped me. Except for my vague, as-yet-inactivated idea of becoming a writer, like many people of my time, I had given up on words like ambition, career, and duty.

I said as much to her.

"But that's quite enough, really, that's perfect. You should just write and not worry about duty and conviction. You don't need to be certain. You don't need to believe. That's one of the things I learned in Warsaw, isn't it, not to believe in anything. The Nazis believed. The Jews believed. And look what happened. Don't bother to believe in any one thing. Just go ahead and write." She reached over and patted my wrist. Then she rested her hand on mine for a second, and then she squeezed and patted my hand again, looking me in the eye.

"You are an engaging young man," she said, still resting her hand on mine.

She had that same steady look that le Baron had—a direct, unblinking stare that seemed to have the ability to penetrate and expose any element of untruth in what you said. It was a look that made me nervous, and, coming from her, with her warm hand still on mine, I wondered—briefly—if I was perhaps being propositioned. I didn't know what to say.

"Never mind," she said. "I've got to go. Peter will be coming back from his spearfishing, and he'll be wondering where I am again."

She stood. Then, smiling sadly, she said something in Polish.

I didn't dare ask her to translate.

From: *The Rose Café*, 2007

Sarah Doublet

Setting: Description of Sarah Doublet, a Native American saunk, or woman leader. She was the last survivor of the Christian Indian people of the Nashobah Plantation village established by the Puritan minister John Eliot in 1640.

...Know ye that I, Sarah Doublett... in Consideration of the sum of five hundred pounds in bills of Credit to me paid and for my benefit and advantage secured by Elnathan Jones, Gentn, and Ephraim Jones, Inholder both of said Concord, fully and absolutely, give, grant, bargain, sell aliene, convey and confirm unto them the said Elnathan Jones, and Ephraim Jones, their heirs and assigns forever in equal shares a certain tract of land lying in Littleton, formerly called Nashobah, in said county of Middlesex by estimation five hundred acres....

–Land grant from the last known surviving Indian
of the Nashobah Plantation to Elnathan and
Ephraim Jones of Concord, September 24, 1736

Sarah Doublet, the original "owner" of the tract, had black eyes and a lurid blue image of a bear tattooed on her left cheek. She tied her long black hair in a knot, fastened with a band of silver, and she dressed in a decorated moose-skin skirt and buskins, with a blue shawl over her shoulders and a beaded blue cloth around her waist. Like all the women of her group, she wore thongs of moose hide around her ankles, and in winter, and sometimes also in summer, she greased her skin with bear fat to keep the cold or the insects at bay.

She was born somewhere in the valley of the Grassy Ground River, probably in the early 1600s, and grew up at the knees of her people, hearing the old stories of the time before the English came. Around age fourteen, when she reached menarche, she was taken away to live alone in a small hut apart from the village, where she cooked her own food or was cared for by crones. The males of her band understood the strong medicine inherent in blood, the force of life, so hunters passing near her hut would avert their eyes, or she hers, her power at this time being too strong for daily life, too poisonous. When her period ended, she was brought back among her people as a woman.

At some point during this same time, she would have gone through a ceremony marking her coming of age, but the details of this, as with so much of the richly textured pattern of the lives of her people, are lost. She married young, had at least two children, lost one in a raid, and then having lost two husbands, married again later in her life, this time to the man known to her people as Nepanet and to the English as Tom Doublet. Before she married, while she was still a virgin, she may have worn long bangs that nearly covered her eyes, or a beaded cap with a fringe over her forehead. But when she married, she swept her hair up into an elaborate coiffure with a knot on the top, the remainder left loose or worn in braids with the bright feathers of blue jays and hawks intertwined within the plaits.

Periodically she would paint herself in blues and reds and don a cloak made of bird feathers or a robe of furred mammal pelts, all hung about with heads and clawed feet and the striped tails of raccoons and skunks and made fast with a belt made from the skin of milk snakes and copperheads. She fixed pendants of swan's-down or shells in her pierced ears, placed a bird-wing headdress in her hair, and strung herself with shell necklaces and ropes of wampum, and perhaps—all this is conjecture— wore an amulet at her breast, a winged thunderbird or the carved image of Ap'cinic, the horned water monster that lived in the depths of the pond below her village.

After *they* came, after she accepted Christianity, she would have ceased to wear bangles and sparkles and fanciful animal skins; she would have cast aside her bird-wing headdress and her swan's-down earrings. She would have become modest, would have lowered her eyes, prayed, sung the strange descant chanting hymns that she and her people would sound out during services. When she was menstruating she would have stayed in the village among the men and no longer would have retreated to the hut in the woods, it being specifically forbidden by the terms of the English contracts that granted her Christianity. According to these terms, she would not weep and tear her hair or smear her face with blood and ash when her fellow tribespeople died, would no longer make a "great noyse by howling" at these times, would not gamble or frolic, would not hold or attend the ceremonial gatherings known as powwows, would not, on pain of death, commit adultery, or pick and eat lice, would not dance, would no longer chant and sing nightlong to the slow hypnotic thrum of the great skin drum. She would wear shoes, would dress her hair in a "comely manner as the English do," would, on the Sabbath, attend church and listen for hours to the long harangues and sermons of her ministers, the descriptions of brimstone and fire and hell, and black-skinned demons with red eyes that fly by night and consume the living flesh of sinners.

By contrast, she would have heard of the mercy of Christ the Redeemer, the everlasting God, the very God of very God, in the language of the as yet- to-be-banned Book of Common Prayer, a god who was begotten, not made, and was of one substance with his Father, God, a Lamb who taketh away the sins of the world, sins of which, by virtue of her birth alone, this Sarah Doublet of Nashobah was guilty.

No matter. Sarah was used to long sermons, harangues, long speeches at her former council meetings. She may even have delivered them herself. She knew the terror that flies by night, the fiery worm, the gnashing devils, and the legends of the tentacled horned monster who would reach up out of the dark waters of Nagog at certain times and draw the entrails of passing villagers down into the depths. She knew the fear of Hobamacho, of night woods, of the screams and howls of her own demons.

She may have been a commoner, an obscure, quiet figure, just one of the fifty to seventy-five people who lived at the Christian Indian village at Nashobah in the fifty years of its existence. She may have been royalty, great-granddaughter of the sachem Tahattawan, who sold Musquetaquid, the Grassy Ground River, to the English. She may have been a leader in her own right, a saunk or "Indian queen" as the English phrased it, who could dispense rights and favors and even land to her people. She may have known the great Queen Wetamoo, who fought the English and had a war camp to the west of Nashobah at Mount Wachusett. Sarah may even have heard, in time of war, the deep-throated throb of Wetamoo's drums. But all that would be later, toward the end. And, in any case, little of any of this is known; it is pieced together from the fragments that I have collected about her and about her people.

From *Trespassing*, 1996

Black Jack Morrison

Setting: The Sarah Doublet Forest

The legal owner of the core of Sarah's tract under the current system of property law is John C. Morrison, whose name you will see inscribed on the records of the deeds of many of the plots of land in the area and who lives in a white farmhouse on the southeastern slope of Nagog Hill. Here, from his prospect, this Morrison, Black Jack Morrison, as he is sometimes called, or Raging Bull, as my friend the Solicitor calls him, the lord of the manor, holds sway. Sometimes he appears on the porch of his manor house, his great barrel chest bared, his hair cropped close in the manner of a Marine sergeant, his thin legs bearing up the great elephantine body, blue eyes piercing at close range, unfocused, as he surveys his holdings: the sweep of the fields down to the pond, the orchard blocks of Macoun, McIntosh, and Northern Spy, the flocks of ducks and geese of which he, John Morrison, Lord of Nashobah, is master.

No one knows the great man, it is said, least of all perhaps those who are closest to him. That is his choice. He bellows at strangers who dare to step into his orchards. He abuses allies and acquaintances, flies into such red rages against his Jamaican pickers that he reduces perfectly strong men to tears. He is a breaker of stallions. He is a hunter of moose and deer and bear, a man of the North Woods and red flannel who will sometimes disappear into lonely hunting camps for weeks at a time, there to brood and drink and kill animals. There are times, it is rumored, when he stalks his land with arms, the great bull neck swelling beneath the collar of his flannel shirt, hunting boots crushing the frozen grass beneath his apple trees, the ice blue eyes searching. Once, the story goes, he shot someone here in the orchard, a trespasser. He was not prosecuted.

One does not prosecute the lord of the manor. The roads passing through the tract are his roads, the geese and ducks he raises on his property are his geese and ducks, the land, *enfin*, is his land. People in the area make a point of avoiding Black Jack Morrison. He is foul-mouthed and abusive, besotted with power, a ranter, a drunk, a violator of local regulations. He proceeds midroad in his golf cart at a leisurely pace, forcing drivers to move slowly behind him in a great slow train. He pulls out onto his roads without watching because they are his roads. He pays his taxes, therefore he owns the roads. By way of penance, a sort of votive candle lit for the town, he serves on the local Appeals board. However, he comes to meetings having consumed more than his normal draft of whiskey and shouts down his opponents. You do not disagree with Mr. John C. Morrison. You do not cut deals with Mr.

John C. Morrison, you do not negotiate, parley, talk of philosophy, of nuance, shades of meaning, music, art, or poetry.

One friend of mine, a woman named Mara, is a literary sort who compares Morrison to the twelfth-century Lord of Hautefort, Bertran de Born, who lived in a castle at Périgueux on a hill above his subjects and went into rages and tirades. He negotiated the fall, it is said, of Henry II, and waged war for the sake of fighting. Ezra Pound says he was a stirrer-up of strife, and the great literary avenger, Dante Alighieri, put him down in Hell and sent him out with his severed head held like a lantern before him.

Such is perhaps the fate of all overbearing landholding lords who abuse their subjects and have no use for local land-use laws. The peasants will rise up, cut off your head, take over your estate, and send you down to Hell.

From: *Trespassing*

First Contact

Setting: Excerpted from the novel, The Last of the Bird People.

A young and ambitious Harvard anthropologist, Minor Randall, discovers a tribe of mixed-race hunter-gatherers living in the wilds of the Swift River Valley in the 1930s, just before the construction of the Quabbin Reservoir, which will destroy the peaceable tribe's forested sanctuary. The story is narrated by an elderly member of the tribe.

The Disappearance of Minor Randall

Précis: This novel, based partly on a true story, is an account and explanation of the abrupt disappearance of the former Harvard anthropologist, Minor Randall, an event that caused a stir in academic circles in the late 1920s.

Randall apparently fell into a controversy with his department head at Harvard because of his involvement with events surrounding the construction of the Quabbin Reservoir.

In the early autumn of 1927, a project surveyor working in the Rattlesnake Brook area in the northern valley found a homemade arrow with a chipped quartz point not far from a hemlock grove on the north-facing slope near a brook. He turned the arrowhead over to his crew boss, who passed it up the chain of command where it eventually ended up at the Harvard Museum of Zoology. After some delays in the upper echelon, it was delivered to Minor Randall for analysis.

The "Rattlesnake Brook Point", as it came to be called, was a mystifying object. For one thing it was related to projectile points used by the Pokanoket tribe in the Cape Cod region during the Contact Period, in the seventeenth century. But it had a number of anomalies which confused Randall, not the least of which was the fact that it was attached to a freshly-stripped hickorywood arrow shaft and was fletched with the feathers of a red-tailed hawk. It was clearly the work of some contemporary individual who had made a lot of arrowheads and knew how to knap stone.

Randall was sufficiently inspired by the workmanship in the arrowhead to do more research. He spent several weeks hiking in the remote, as yet unsurveyed sections of the valley, searching for more artifacts. At the end of this period, he discovered a deerskin cap decorated with grouse feathers. Later that fall, in the mud beside Rattlesnake Brook, he found the barefooted print of a child. He subsequently came to believe that there was a group of aboriginal people living somewhere in the valley.

Below is an account of his first meeting with a tribal member, Chanterelle, his future paramour.

NB: By this point in the novel, the Bird People, know Randall has been tracking them. They begin to call him the "Tracker."

The novel is told as a court deposition of the events that took place in the year after the so-called tribe of "gypsies" burned the construction equipment of the workers clearing the forests for the Quabbin Reservoir. The story is told by an elderly member of the tribe, an unreliable narrator.

Tracker Randall first came to our valley in autumn the year before we set the fire. He was a Wasichu unlike any other Wasichu man. He had sand-colored hair and dressed in sand-colored clothes. He was smaller than most Wasichus, and unlike the others, he slept in the forest at night. He ate the same plants we ate, and once, before we captured him, we saw him kill a rabbit with a stone.

We knew from the start he was following us. And of course as we have done ever since we were born by Jenna Crow, when we first saw him we became birds so that he would not know that we were living in the Wasichu people's forest—or what they believed was their forest.

Many nights we laughed at the efforts of this Wasichu man we came to call the Tracker. And then when winter came, he went away, and then we laughed even more. But when spring came, he returned. This time he was as regular as the rising sun. He waited for days in our best plant gathering grounds, watching for us. He left the toys of his people for us to take away, presents or gifts to trick us. But we would not be tricked. We had enough. We carried with us all that we needed to live in our world—the bow and the arrow, the spear, the nets, and the skinning knife, the awl, the baskets, and the fish line and the birdbone hooks and stone sinkers.

So when the Tracker left decorative beads for us, and more knives, and shining glass, what did we do? We threw these things aside, laughing, although I will say that one day, as a joke, Three Birds squatted over one of the mirrors and soiled it with her waters and left it there for Tracker Randall to pick up again.

Chanterelle is the one who finally brought this Tracker among us. She had come across his spoor, and many times, contrary to the teachings of our people, she followed after him just to see what he was doing out there on our land. Sometimes, although not often, because she had no man of her own except that pest Watson, I knew she had experienced longings for some other man, someone unlike any man she had ever known. And even though she knew the Tracker would kill her if he saw her, she thought sometimes of him as a man. And not a Wasichu.

And just then, deep in the sunless chasm, she stopped. She knew he had come.

She dared not turn to look, because she knew she was about to die. But nothing happened, and so after a time she turned her head very slowly and saw the Tracker standing there in the half light, just at the edge of the grove, his mouth open like some slow-witted woodchuck who does not understand the meaning of life.

For some reason the Tracker did not attempt to kill her. He merely stared at her, as if he had never seen a real human being before.

And then came the biggest surprise.

He spoke in our language to Chanterelle. Not the language we now speak, but the ancient language of our people. He was a Wasichu man, but he knew the formal language of the council, the words we took from the old way, before the time of Jenna Crow.

Even I did not know how he could have had knowledge of that secret language.

Chanterelle was gone in a breeze, a swirl of dust. But she came back. And now she came with drawn bow, and he who was about to die, who was close to feeling the firestab of an arrow in his chest, cried out in the old language again and said things like, "Pookon naskue? What is your name? and "Noksu whasta" I am friend, and for this reason Chanterelle faltered and eased off the bowstring.

And so the two of them stood there looking at each other, she in her dogskin skirt and he in his sand-colored clothes and the thin, golden-colored spectacles he always wore.

She drew the bow again slowly this time. Then, gnashing her teeth and hissing and growling at him, she backed away toward the river, out of the oak grove, while he watched, mouth still open.

This time there was no question that he had seen her, that he knew that there was at least one wild forest creature living in the valley. So after that, even though we argued about the idea for five nights straight, we had no choice. We had to catch him.

From: *The Last of the Bird People,* 2012

The Great God Pan

Précis: On a hike in the foothills of the Cévennes mountains in Provence, I have an inexplicable encounter.

Pan was born in Arcadia in the remote valleys and highlands where shepherds tended their flocks. He was the son of the nymph Penelope (not the wife of Odysseus, a different Penelope). His father may have been no less a figure than Zeus, although Apollo figures in some myths, and Hermes is also a major contender, since he was very much at home in Arcadia. In fact there is a rumor that all of Penelope's various suitors managed to introduce some genetic material into this decidedly earthy god—the Greek word pan means "all." But it is more likely that his name is a contraction of the root word *paon*, which means herdsman and is the root of the English and Romance language word "pasture."

The lower half of Pan's body was goat— shaggy limbs and hooves—but he had the upper body and face of a man, except for a billy goat beard and horns. In other words, Pan embodied a Medieval devil image. Penelope fled in terror, it is said, when she first saw the baby she had produced. Pan is often confused with satyrs, who had a similar appearance, but the satyrs apparently began as humans and became animals, whereas Pan was mostly animal. He sounds a great deal like Gilgamesh's good friend Enkidu, who was a half-human, half-forest creature. The big difference is that Enkidu was seduced by a woman and became more human, whereas Pan was a great lecher who seems to have been unconcerned about who he mated with—nymphs, goddesses, shepherdesses, other goats, and even, via nightmares, nineteenth-century women.

Like his predecessor, Enkidu, he is associated with wild nature and inhabits that untamed zone of forest and rock just beyond the village boundary, where he cavorts with his fellow travelers, the satyrs and nymphs. Out there, in this legendary danger zone, the wild, or the unhoused wilderness that haunted the nightmares of European villagers for a thousand years, he is everywhere, and while you are in his domain, anything—a breaking branch, a sudden rush of wind, or here in the Americas the whirring break of a surprised grouse—will bring him to you in the form of panic (from the Greek word *panikos*, meaning "of Pan").

That's the thing about Pan. You don't always see him, or if you do, he will cause you to forget the incident, as he did with Ratty and Mole. Sometimes though, according to folklore, you can smell him, the randy odor of a horny goatman. And sometimes—often I think—you feel him. You go out to some wild place, some remote rocky hillside, a rushing falls, a deep glen, and you stand there in awe, and then something hits you, a sense that you are being watched, that you are not alone, and that something terrifying could happen here in this god-haunted site, this sacred patch of earth. That too is Pan.

I think I saw him once, years ago. I was taking a little walkabout in the Cévennes Mountains in the south of France and came across one of those ferny ravines with a fresh stream running through. It was hot, I had been walking for a while, and this fresh, bubbling stream, the shaded glen, and the mossy bank offered a cooling respite, so I took off my shoes, soaked my feet for a while, and then lay back on the bank. I fell into one of those dreamy half-sleeps there. I was dozing, but I still could hear clearly the riffles of the brook and, beyond the ravine, the high, incessant shushing sound of the cicadas, and far off, somewhere beyond the high walls, the distant clang of goatbells. Maybe I fell asleep and dreamed what came next, but suddenly there was a little cascade of rocks, I opened my eyes, and in the brush across the stream I saw a hideous, bearded goatlike face, with loose lips, great curling horns, and a human nose and mouth. I sat up abruptly and the thing, whatever it was, disappeared. I heard the clatter of loosed stones again, as if the beastman were scrambling up the ravine slope. And then the sounds of the brook returned; and the loud pulsing of the cicadas seemed to increase until it filled the whole hollow.

I presumed this was one of the many goats that range through this part of the world, but when I crossed the brook I saw no goat sign. In fact, I couldn't find any indication that there had been any animal there at all.

The Cévennes region is rich in ruins. Everywhere I went I came across the remnants of one of the various cultures that had existed in this part of the world over the last two thousand years—nineteenth-century farm-houses, Medieval Christian churches, ruined monasteries, Roman walls and towers, even a prehistoric artifact or two. In the dry valleys and hills, there was still an aura of the classic pastoral, and there were many little herds of goats and sheep—you could almost always hear their bells on the distant slopes, and sometimes toward evening you could hear the sharp whistles and shouts of the goatherds bringing down the flocks for the evening milking. I could not shake the thought that I had seen something other than a goat, and that I had seen this face before somewhere.

From: *The Wildest Place on Earth*, 2015

A Sacrilegious Bee

Setting: While researching the gardens of Rome I meet a gentle elderly priest.

I remember an old priest I met in Rome some years after this encounter. He was seated on a fallen pillar near the Forum reading his Missal. I saluted him as I passed and he too engaged me in conversation. We chatted briefly, in a civil manner, about ancient Rome, about certain emperors, the good ones, and the bad ones, his family in the mountains, flowers, birds, the weather, America, and all manner of things. But oddly enough, even though he was a man of the cloth, there was not one word of religion.

At one point he said he came here every day to sit on the fallen pillars of the past, beneath the umbrella pines, to read his prayer book and enjoy "the beauties of nature"—such as they were in that busy beehive city.

He seemed anxious to talk, so I asked him if he had had a good life as a priest.

"Oh yes, very good life, but then from where I come, you have not many choices. You grow olives and potatoes, you drive a delivery truck, you leave the village and work in the industries, you go to Germany, or you do as I have done, and you become a priest and you lead a little flock of sheep over the barren hills, and then, as I am doing, you prepare your soul for Heaven."

Then he asked me why I had come to Rome and did I enjoy Italy, and I tried to explain, as best I could, my interest in gardens and my quest to recover that sense of wildness, that spirit of wild nature that I once had known.

"Oh but young man," he said, tapping his chest with his fist, "you are looking in the wrong site. The wildest place on earth, it is here, in the human heart."

I am not sure of the cosmic significance of what followed, but for no apparent reason that I could determine, a bee came winging over my shoulder at that point, flew straight for the priest and unceremoniously, in an entirely irreligious act, stung him on the cheek. He laughed and brushed it away.

"Did it hurt?" I asked.

"No, no, I am used to bee stings. We kept bees at the monastery. I think the bee is an animal with a very long memory. We stole so much of their honey, now word must have gotten around: "Sting all gentlemen in black robes."

"Well, I hope they're done with their revenge for now," I said, and bid him farewell.

From: "The Wildest Place on Earth," 2001

Robin Hood in America

Setting: Sherwood Forest

It was springtime in Nottingham and all through Sherwood Forest the bluebells were in bloom and the woods were alive with the song of the cuckoo, thrush, and wood pigeon. On this particular day, there came riding through the overarching oaks and beeches a certain knight in black armor, his lance lowered and his visor cocked up on his forehead. As he rounded the bend, the knight saw, pulled across the track, a cart loaded with a barrel of wine and two rough-looking chaps accompanied by a portly monk in nut brown robes. The knight reigned in his Friesian stallion and snapped up his lance.

"Clear the way, hedge pigs," he shouted. "By what right are you here in the King's forest? Account yourselves."

The goodly friar took it upon himself to engage the knight in a debate on the matter of access.

"But my liege, we are in fact the legal residents of Sherwood Forest," he said, "and we reserve the right to question any man who passeth this way."

"And from whom dost thou hold this right, if I might be so bold as to inquire?" asked the knight. He was clearly unimpressed by his adversaries.

"Of one Robin Hood, a gentleman of whom ye may have heard," said the friar.

"I have indeed heard of the man, who has not? But never have I heard the term 'gentleman' applied to said knave. Moreover, I believe that this forest belongs to King John—the trees, the underwood, and also the streams and the boar and the deer to boot." The goodly friar stepped forward and held up his hand, index and middle finger raised as if in benediction.

"True," he said, "this wood is the realm of the king, but *Deo volente*, the forest is also the domain of Robin Hood." The knight adjusted his visor and chuckled cynically.

"And how came this to pass?" he asked with mock formality.

"Explained plainly, Sir Knight, my argument runneth thus. God may have bestowed this forest on King John, but *de facto* God did also grant these lands to Robin Hood. Likewise to all people hereabout. That is to say, we hold this land by divine right. The King, being human—and hardly divine—is beholden also to the Almighty; and being human and therefore profane hath no more rights than any man who walks the earth as far as the use of Sherwood Forest is concerned."

This little exchange—a scene pieced together from various ballads, minstrel songs, plays, and novels—represents the heart of the argument of the whole body of the Robin Hood story cycle: the question of the use of land. It is a dispute that began long before Robin Hood and one that has carried on ever since his time. It involves, along with the unequal distribution of wealth, one of the most basic conflicts of the human experience: the control of land, which until fairly recently in history was one and the same with the control of capital.

In Robin Hood's time, the late twelfth century, there was indeed a great deal of strife among the king and the commoners and barons over the use of formerly common land. The issue was rooted in land controls known as the Forest Laws, a new system established by William the Conqueror in the late eleventh century. The crown in those days (and still today, in theory) owned all of England, including the deer and the boar and the salmon in the streams. But until William's Forest Laws were instituted, the peasantry was able to utilize what was known as the vert and venison, that is, the plants and animals of the forest. In fact, the deer and the boar, the berries, nuts, and mushrooms, were a major resource for the cottagers and villeins of feudal England. For 500 years after the arrival of William the Conqueror, the populace resented and, as with Robin Hood, sometimes resisted, the king's edicts.

Robin was not the last of the forest rebels. Over the centuries, as laws of the land evolved, other

Robin Hood-like figures have arisen to preserve the public access to common land, and more recently to protect, by whatever means possible, the local ecosystems.

Here in the Americas, a 200-year-long running battle with the native people, known as the Indian Wars, was fought over more or less the same issue that Robin Hood dealt with—eviction from commonly held lands. In the United States, where the doctrine of private property was definitively established in the Fifth Amendment of the American Constitution, the resistance continued In the eighteenth century in Maine, a group of homesteaders were threatened with eviction by distant land-holders; and in reaction, calling themselves The White Indians, rose up to defend their use of the land. The same thing happened along the Hudson River in the nineteenth century, when a band of local farmers known as the Calico Boys countered the feudal dictates of the vast holdings of the Van Rennselaer family.

But it was in the late 1960s and early 1970s that some of the most radical Robin-Hood like environmental activists rose up in defense of natural resources.

Inspired in part by Edward Abbey's popular 1975 novel *The Monkey Wrench Gang,* David Foreman and a group called Earth First! used industrial sabotage as a means of protecting land. Other back-to-the-land environmentalists such as Doug Peacock, who was the model for one of Edward Abbey's characters, took to the woods and lived side by side (more or less) with grizzly bears. Julia Butterfly Hill, in one of the more extreme and imaginative acts of environmental resistance, lived in a redwood tree for more than two years in order to save it from foresters.

But it was the father of them all, Edward Abbey, who was the most Robin Hood-like of them in spirit. In his arguments for the preservation of the southern Utah wilderness, he argued, as did Robin Hood, that uncultivated land should be the property of all people. "Keep it wild," he said.

Robin Hood, were he with us now, would surely understand.

From: *Sanctuary*

The Wrath of the Wild Bull

Setting: Out looking for blue-grey gnatcatchers in a deciduous woodlot across the road from my house, a place I have been visiting for nearly thirty years, I meet an angry developer.

After wandering around a bit looking into the tree tops and listening for their call I spent the rest of the morning, mostly sitting quietly on a large boulder on the southwestern part of the woods, away from the brook. I saw a number of local birds there, a catbird, a towhee, a few buzzing little warblers that I couldn't see well enough to identify, and also a yellow warbler and a Maryland yellowthroat. Also woodpeckers, bluejays, a finch, and a few other common species, but no blue-gray gnatcatchers. I decided to give up and go home for breakfast.

Just as I was exiting the woods and stepping out into the field, I saw a large Mercedes SUV pass by, stop, and back up. A blond, heavyset man got out of the car and crossed the field toward me with a clearly determined stride, like a bull.

I waited.

His opening salvo made things all too clear.

"Private Property!" he said.

He wanted to know what the hell I was doing there in the woods.

As a seasoned trespasser, I have learned to read the character of those who feel it necessary, for one reason or another, to inform me that their land is private land. I could see where this man was going and in order to defuse him, I played the part of a somewhat slow and innocent bird watcher.

"I was looking for blue-gray gnatcatchers," I said. "They are beautiful little birds, very rare, do you know them ?"

He didn't answer.

"That's private property, OK? That woods; you can't go in there."

"Private property?"

"Yeah, private. Keep out."

"But these are Charlie's fields. He used to graze his heifers here. One of them escaped a few years ago," I said.

"Well whoever Charlie is he don't own that land."

"Terribly sorry, I thought it was Charlie's, the old farmer," I said. "You see I walk here daily on my circuit, looking for birds. There are some beautiful and rare species here. For example, if you come to these fields and the low woodland there in March, you can witness the haunting and beautiful mating dance of the woodcock."

"Yeah, well don't go in there, and get off this land. You live around here?"

"Yes, I am the groundskeeper for the Vicarage Garden, a sanctuary for birds. We get some very interesting species of birds there. Also crickets.

But no blue-gray gnatcatchers, so you see I make a circuit through these lands. They're all a part of Scratch Flat, and I am researching the various species of birds and mammals that occur here. I have seen bobcats in the woods there. Mountain lions. Black bears." (All that part was true.) "I could show you around if you'd like."

By this time the man, whoever he was, had calculated that he was dealing with a slightly off-center individual, possibly feeble- minded, and he grew kinder.

"You're not supposed to go in that woods anymore," he said.

"But why not? I've been walking there all these years, searching for rare species. I saw a hooded warbler in there last year. Also a prothonatory warbler!"

"I'm sorry," he said "But you can't go there anymore. I am buying that property."

"You own it?"

"Not yet."

"But Charlie likes to have me walk there. Some years ago he lost a heifer. I personally think one of the mountain lions or one of the wolf packs got her. But Charlie, you know, he's older now and imagines things. He thinks the calf is still in there, and she has gone wild—like one of the so-called wild cattle. Have you heard of them? Back in the old days in the South, in the Great Dismal Swamp in Virginia, cows would go wild. Escaped slaves lived there and hunted them. Charlie wants me to keep an eye for her."

"That right?" the buyer said, kindly.

"Well, yes. I mean I don't believe Charlie. I think the poor heifer got eaten."

"Really?"

"Yes."

I didn't mention that this "Charlie," the original owner, had died three years earlier.

"Listen, pal don't go in there anymore, alright. I don't want you to get hurt, or eaten by one of them mountain lions, OK? Please don't go there."

"Don't go in the woods?" I asked, as if he had said 'stop breathing'.

"Not those woods. Private Property."

"I know a man who lives in Concord, and he told me there is no such thing as private property."

"Well he's wrong. Don't believe that man. And stay out. I'll have to tell the police if I see you in there again."

"The police? Why the police?" I asked in all innocence.

"Yes, it's illegal to walk there now. Can you understand that?"

I looked back at the woods, then looked at him, and shrugged, dumb-founded.

"Don't go there," he said with definitive finality.

He turned and marched back to his car.

I was tempted to tell him that he had not actually seen me in the woods and therefore could not legally charge me with trespassing. And in fact if he did not "own" the land yet, how could he forbid me to walk there? But since he seemed to be the buyer and (presumably) the developer, I held my fire. There would surely be more public confrontations to come.

Of course, threats of trespassing charges notwithstanding, I went back to the woods the next day, and again the day after. But when I went back the following week the property was surrounded by "No Trespassing" signs.

And thus the woods became "The Forbidden Forest", which of course, made it all the more enticing.

From: *The Garden at the End of Time,* 2025

Forbidden Waters

Setting: Skinny dipping in Concord's reservoir.

On the point of land now held by the Concord Water Department, which once had a big summer house at the site, there is a rocky shoreline that provides access to the forbidden waters.

As I moved out onto the point, I heard quiet laughter, then a great splash and outflow of breath, and came upon three teenagers, two girls and a young man, skinny-dipping in Concord's drinking water.

As a fellow trespasser and objective observer, I felt this was none of my business, and turned to retreat and nearly crashed into a fourth teenager carrying a case of beer to the site.

"Sorry, man," he said after a torrent of surprised expletives.

"Don't worry, I'm not the police," I said.

Then I asked him if he came here often and if he had ever seen other people here at night on the other side of the road

"Yeah," he said. "You see weirdos sometimes."

"Weirdos?"

"You know, like weirdos. Freaks."

By now the swimmers had spotted us, and having dressed or at least covered themselves, and having determined that I was not an authority, joined in.

"You know, really weird," one said.

"Like, you know, men with glasses. Geeks."

"Nerds?" I asked.

"No, not nerds exactly, geeks, like really weird," one of the girls joined in enthusiastically.

"One night, we were here, and, like, there was this guy, and he, like, looked at us, and then he like went off into the woods, and he didn't say hello, or what are you guys doing here, or anything. He was so—like—weird."

"He looked at you?"

"Yeah, weirdly. It freaked me. You know, he just like-looked."

"I remember that guy," her boyfriend said. "A geek with glasses."

"Then there was this other guy," she said, "remember him? Some kind of dude with a box."

"That was a fisherman."

"No, no, there was a weirdo with a box, and he had like body parts in it that he was going to throw in the pond, so the cops couldn't find it."

"Body parts?" I asked

"It was just some kind of fisherman, Tracy, it wasn't a guy with body parts."

"She always sees this stuff," another said.

"No, I could sense it. He was weird," she said. "It was his wife or something. You know, like that guy who sang in the church choir and then killed his wife."

"That was a long time ago, Trace. Don't listen to her, none of this is true."

"There was a guy in the choir, and he like killed his wife when she was out running, right near here, too. My parents knew him, and he was really weird, sang in the choir and went to church, then he kills people and puts their body parts in coolers and pretends to go fishing."

"They say Indians are coming here, back in the hills across the road there, and leaving things," I told them.

"What do you mean?" Tracy asked. "Like body parts and stuff?"

"No, just things-sticks, brush, stones, pine cones."

"Why would they want to do that?" they asked.

"They say it is their way of honoring the place. They're trying to get back to their old religion."

"So they leave like sticks around?" Tracy asked.

"Yes, sticks. I've found pine cones placed in the crotches of trees, things like that."

"You mean like stick sticks?" she asked.

"Yes."

"Talk about weird," she said.

There actually was a dark event at this spot back in the 1920s, but given the discussion of body parts, and the slim, cloud-filtered, quarter moon, the half-naked younger generation, and the presence of a man such as myself, who, I am sure, would be the subject of much conversation and teenage folklore for many months to come, I decided not to tell them.

On such a night in August in the late 1920s, a local swain, who could not have been much more than a teenager himself, was rowing his girlfriend on the dark waters of Nagog. Somewhere, somehow, between the island and the western shore, where the teenagers and I were now standing, this woman, Virginia Mills, fell, or was pushed, from the boat. She had a flashlight in her hand at the time, and as she sank beneath the water, her companion, or paramour, or whoever he was, saw the light sinking, an eerie gleam, descending deeper and deeper below the surface. Later that night the rescuers saw the faint glow and found her body.

The whole thing was reminiscent of Theodore Dreiser's *An American Tragedy*, which was published in 1925 and would have been known at the time of this incident. One wonders whether it was a question of life imitating art.

The presence of uncouth teenagers, bathing and, for all I know, relieving themselves in the waters of the good people of Concord, made me think I should, after all, do something for the community, so I told the teenagers the story of Sarah Doublet and the horned water monster that the Indians believed lurked in the deeper parts of the pond.

"It had these long tentacles, they say, and a huge gnashing beak and horns on its head. At night it would reach up and feel along the shore for people, fishermen, swimmers, things like that. If it caught you, it would either drag you down into the waters, or worse, slice you open and suck out your intestines."

The teenagers were quiet for a minute.

"You mean it would like eat you alive?" Tracy asked.

"Yeah, suck out your inner body parts while you clung to a tree."

"Cool," she said.

From: *Trespassing*, 1996

The Discovery of Europe

Setting: The Vatican. In a reversal of Columbus Day, a Native-American man "discovers" Europe.

On September 23, 1973, Adam Fortunate Eagle of the Chippewa Nation crossed the Atlantic Ocean and discovered Italy.

Even before he set foot on Italian soil, news of Fortunate Eagle's impending arrival had spread among the natives. He had announced to a representative of the Italian nation, a certain Signor Squadrille of the Italian consulate, his intended voyage of discovery, and the Italian people, in particular the Italian press, were ready and waiting. On September 23, 1973, "Chief Joseph," the great silver bird carrying Fortunate Eagle and his entourage, descended from the clouds and landed upon flat ground beyond a beautiful Italian city known to the local people as Rome.

Knowing he would encounter native inhabitants, perhaps savage, Adam Fortunate Eagle had arrayed himself in traditional American dress. He wore a fringed buckskin war shirt, a silver turquoise ring, a palette of human hair (he once had symbolically scalped his enemy Columbus), and a variety of feathers from American birds. In his right hand he carried a ceremonial spear. The natives were excited when he appeared; the local reporters swarmed around him, fawning, but he strode through the crowd and, raising his spear, drove it into Italian soil, thus claiming the land for the Chippewas.

"Take me to your leader," he said.

The next day he was led to a grand palace. He ascended a wide flight of marble stairs and was ushered into a spacious room where a small dark man in a grey suit was sitting. The small man rose and greeted Adam Fortunate Eagle warmly. Fortunate Eagle was informed through interpreters that this was Giovanni Leone, the current Chief, or President, of the Italian nation. The two chatted amicably, and while they talked a message was delivered by a page. An important spiritual leader, a man known as "The Pope," had heard of the arrival of Fortunate Eagle and wished to pay homage to the great explorer.

At eleven o'clock the following morning, Adam Fortunate Eagle entered into the Vatican, a grand city within a city. He saw before him a pleasing arrangement of basilicas, chapels, libraries, piazzas, and colonnades—a collection of buildings equal, nearly, to the great cities of the American natives: Teotihuacán, Tikal, Tenochtitlán, and the mountain city of the Incas, Machu Picchu. Inside the temples of Rome there were stained glass windows, and vast frescoes of unclothed human beings with wings arched across the ceilings; there were domes and marble floors and grand interior vistas.

Fortunate Eagle was conducted by an entourage of splendidly costumed officials into an inner sanctum where the spiritual leader held court. Soon a heavy studded door opened at the end of a hall, and a man in white silken vestments and a conical hat came forward and greeted him. Adam Fortunate Eagle was informed that this was the famous Pope.

The Pope held out his hand, indicating that Fortunate Eagle should kiss his ring. The discoverer of Italy stared indignantly at the hand of this poseur and then held out his ring, the silver one, with the precious turquoise stone, indicating through sign that the Pope should kiss it. Instead, smiling broadly, the Pope took his hand and held it while the two of them spoke of their two nations. Speaking in English, and with a certain understanding and genuine sympathy, the Pope said he could feel in his heart the plight of the Chippewa people at the hands of the occupying government of America. Adam Fortunate Eagle was moved by his sympathy.

"Thank you, my son," he said.

Adam Fortunate Eagle returned to the Americas and announced his discovery. But, other than a flurry of interest in the national press, what is certainly the greatest event in Chippewa history has gone unnoticed.

From: Essay, 1992

PART TWO: A SENSE OF PLACE

Scratch Flat

Setting: Scratch Flat, the square mile of agricultural land that served as the setting for six future books.

There is a plum grove just above the house in which I live, a tangled, unproductive group of some twelve trees that were planted sometime in the late 1920s by an old curmudgeon who lived in the house in the decades following the turn of the century. Every morning between April and November, weather permitting, I take a pot of coffee up to that grove to watch the sun come up over the lower fields and to think about things. More and more now I find myself thinking there about time, how it drifts in from the future, how it brushes past us briefly in the present, and then drifts off again to become the past, and how none of these stages, neither past, nor present, nor future, is really knowable. Presented with this dilemma, I have come in recent years to accept the primitive concept of ceremonial time, in which past, present, and future can all be perceived in a single moment, generally during some dance or sacred ritual. Ceremonial time was perceived easily by the people who lived on the land around the plum grove for most of human history. The Nipmuck Indians would summon it up regularly during certain periods of the year, and I have found that it is a convenient method of understanding the changes that have taken place on this particular patch of earth over the last fifteen thousand years.

I should say at the outset, since this is a book about time and place, that history hangs heavily in this area. Fifteen thousand years ago the last of three glacial advances smoothed the rough edges of a small patch of land about ten miles north of the Concord River. After the glacier retreated, it left behind on that particular section of land a deep bed of sand and gravel which, in subsequent centuries, was overlaid with a rich layer of topsoil. Even before the last ice of the glacier had melted from the barren, rolling hills, small bands of fur-clad hunters, known technically as Paleo-Indians, moved into the region in search of game. In due time, that is, after some five thousand years, the descendants of these Paleo people settled into semipermanent villages, some of which were located not far from the square-mile tract of land in question. A thousand years ago these Indians, who by now had organized themselves into a tribe known as the Pawtuckets, found that by clearing off some of the existing vegetation in the area and replacing it with other plants, the production of food could be substantially increased. This revolutionary development gave birth to an agricultural economy which has survived on that little section of earth ever since.

Five or six centuries after the Pawtucket agricultural experiments began, a group of new settlers moved into the region and improved on the technique. These newcomers had white skin and brought with them from Europe new crops, exotic animals, and an attitude toward the land that, in the space of a few decades, altered the entire environment. Whereas in 1630 the area had been characterized by deep woods broken only by a few primitive garden clearings, by 1790 the land consisted, for the most part, of open, rolling fields of English hay, rough grazing meadows, orchards, and large kitchen gardens.

The white settlers who moved into the area also constructed a new kind of shelter. In contrast to the rounded wickiups of the Pawtuckets, these were squared-off, framed structures designed to keep the natural world at bay. By 1850, there were about seven of these buildings in the little patch of land that the glacier scraped off. One of these, a small farmhouse, was constructed on an east-facing slope by a farmer named Peter Farwell. About one hundred fifty years later, I moved into that house and as a result have come to know and love the square-mile tract of land that surrounds it.

My understanding of this land is circumscribed by time as we measure it here in the West. I seem almost always to be stuck in this little slice of history we call the present, but there are days, there are periods, when some obscure combination of forces seems to release an awareness of ceremonial time so I can see the history of this little stretch of land in sharpened detail. Invariably on these days I get up from my chair in the plum grove and begin to walk, and invariably I seem to cover a certain territory on these walks, not unlike a dog or a bird. It is bordered on the south by a highway, known locally as the Great Road, which runs from Concord, Massachusetts, north-north-west to the small villages of southern New Hampshire. The Great Road was originally an Indian trail which meandered through what is now known as the Nashoba Valley. In its recent history, the road carried a number of important personages and was involved in a small, obscure way, in national events. For sixty or seventy years, the brightest and the best in the American establishment traveled on this highway between Groton School and Harvard University in Cambridge. And one April morning in the late eighteenth century, a group of militant farmers marched down the Great Road to a bridge over the Concord River to start a revolution. But all that is another story.

To the east and north, the territory in question is bordered by a stream known as Beaver Brook which the glacier gouged out during its retreat. It is a pleasant little body of water, offering clear, and in places, deep waters for swimming and good courses for skating in winter. In any other part of the world, Beaver Brook might be termed a river; it is slow-flowing and deep in some sections, and in places it widens to 50 yards or more. As do most of the rivers in the region south of the Merrimack River, the brook flows northward. Its wide grassy marshes provide excellent habitat for ducks, geese, otters, muskrat, as well as a few rarer species of plants and animals. The brook curves westward at the northern end of its course and empties into a shallow lake which the early white settlers called Forge Pond. The waters of this lake are relatively clean and swimmable, and fishermen still seem to find something worth casting for there in spite of the fact that in recent years it has been surrounded with the habitations of modern-day Americans. The houses are of a type that were built originally as summer cottages and then later winterized for permanent dwellings. On a point of land, so far undeveloped, on the southeast shore of the lake, the Pawtucket Indians and their progenitors would hold festivals and, if my sources are accurate, the normal flow of time as we now measure it, would stop, run backward, or collapse altogether so that the primal shamans of who knows how many generations, the spirits of dead bears and wolves, would come alive again and dance there in the half-lit regions between the firelight and the forest wall.

The western edge of the tract of land is bordered by a deep pine forest and a brooding larch swamp. Whippoorwills nest in the pine forest, and although I rarely see them, I can often hear barred owls, great horned owls, and screech owls calling from the darkened interior. On the east side of that pine forest and about an eighth of a mile behind my house, there is a grove of very old hemlock trees. Some of the trees in the grove are hollowed and broken, some may have been standing in the years when local rabble-rousers in the community were mobilizing against the British; and the general sense of the place is gloomy and dark, as if some unspeakable acts took place there, some brutal rite whose aura has been carried forward into the twentieth century. As you will see, this may or may not be the case, but I will come to that in due time.

Just south of the pine woods there is a wide field that is usually planted in corn by Matty Matthews, a hardworking dairy farmer who is determined to continue farming in spite of the fact that economies of this region appear to be working against him. Just south of Matthews's cornfield, you will come again to the Great Road. There are five farms in this square-mile tract, four of which are located on the main highway. Next to the Matthews place there is a 120-acre spread known as Sherman's Acres which, in recent years, has sprouted a lucrative crop of suburban tract houses. East of Sherman's there is a farm run by a Greek immigrant named Jimmy-George Starkos, which is by far the most pleasant and the best-tended of the five farms in the square-mile tract. Jimmy-George's farm is made up of beet and bean fields which rise up to a wooded ridge to the east. Beyond the ridge there is another farm which, for more than eighty years, housed local paupers and transients. The house is still there, but a few years ago the farmer sold off his hayfields to developers and now there are several large, flat buildings on the land, owned for the most part by computer companies. The place was once known as Beaver Brook Farm; now it is called—without a touch of conscious irony—Beaver Brook Industrial Park.

Walk north of the industrial park along the banks of Beaver Brook and you will come full circle. There is a stretch of oak and pine woods owned by a local sportsmen's club (again, no irony in the name) and just to the north you will come to a group of fields which are more or less central to this story. For one thing, this particular farm lies at the center of the square-mile tract that I am describing, and for another, a lot of history has been played out in that 200 acres of old fields and woods. The property is owned by a man named Charlie Lignos who owns a dairy farm in the next town and who, for some obscure reason, is allowing perfectly good agricultural land to grow up to woods. The farm consists of some five fields, each separated by stone walls and hedgerows. The fields rise up from Beaver Brook in a series of terraces and are interspersed with untended apple orchards and patches of dense woods. The soil is good in the area and in all likelihood, given the location, the land has been farmed for more than five hundred years, first by the Pawtuckets, then by Christianized Indians, and then finally by white Europeans.

A man named Jeremiah Caswell was the first European to work this land; in the mid-eighteenth century he cleared most of the tract, planted orchards, and unlike his Indian predecessors, brought in livestock—oxen, dairy cows, pigs, goats, and later horses and sheep. In 1973 there were three barns and three houses associated with the original Caswell holdings; by 1979 there were only two structures left. Vandals had burned two barns and an abandoned house, and the town had torn down the third barn because, officials said, it was an attractive nuisance, an indication, in my opinion, of the economic direction that the community is taking. The main house, the old Caswell estate, has been restored and is now surrounded by extensive flower gardens. The four acres of land surrounding the other Caswell house are being farmed once more in an odd sort of way, but the house itself, although sturdy enough, is in continual need of repair; I know this for a fact, since I am the one who lives there.

During the brighter years in this town, that is, during the height of the nineteenth-century agricultural period, the square-mile section of land which I have described was called Scratch Flat. One local legend suggests that Scratch Flat was so named because in the 1860s a number of families living there suffered from a "certain cutaneous itch" for seven years. More likely the tract got its name from the fact that the flat land surrounding a low hill in the area was so thoroughly cultivated. Whereas the rest of the community was known for its apple and pear orchards, Scratch Flat was always known for its good soil and its truck farms. My friend Margaret Lacey, a ninety-five-year-old woman who had ice blue eyes and a long memory, told me that on summer nights during the 1890s the air in Scratch Flat was heavy with the smell of celery, and even up to the 1950s the area was known for its farms. Billy Sherman used to be called the Cauliflower King by the buyers in the Haymarket in Boston, and Jimmy-George Starkos sent three sons to college on the money earned from a roadside stand which was open only four months of the year.

All of them, Starkos, Sherman, Caswell, and the Pawtuckets, can thank the glacier for their success in life. The deep bed of sand and gravel, the easy slopes, the drainage patterns, and the deep layer of organic topsoil made it easy to farm in this area. It is no accident that the industrial development that swept through New England during the nineteenth century skipped over Scratch Flat and the valley in which the town is located. On the other hand, the same factors that make the land good for farming also make it good for housing and modern industrial development; and, in spite of the good soil, in spite of the fact that arable land is something of a rare commodity in New England, more and more now, computer companies and new houses are appearing on the farmlands of the town.

From *Ceremonial Time: Fifteen Thousand Years on One Square Mile,* 1984

Place and Remembrance

Setting: The Palisades, New York

The great American naturalist Edwin Way Teale believed that up until recently most people had some lonely spot where they could get away from it all, a little woodlot or streambank that engrained itself in the child's mind so that even in adulthood the place would endure in memory as an almost mystic domain, an enchanted spot somewhere at a remove from current existence.

I had a spot of that sort. Whose place it was, I never knew. The old estate building had burned, or was torn down or otherwise destroyed, and all that remained was the sad foundation and an apron of broken tiles that once served as a terrace, now overgrown with grass and struggling maple seedlings.

Beyond the terrace was a boxwood hedge gone wild and a shallow garden pool of broken moss-covered stone. The whole ruined garden was surrounded by a rich mid-Atlantic forest—great columns of sweet gum, beech, and tulip. And scattered within the gloom of the overarching trees were standing pergolas, broken pillars, the ruins of a garden house, and, most intriguing of all, an ancient swimming pool with a large puddle of standing water at the deep end, greenish with algae, occupied by golden-eyed frogs that dipped beneath the shadowy waters long before you could even think about catching them.

The ruins were perched on red cliffs high above the gray Hudson River.

I later learned the site was one of many such estates that had lined the cliffs in the bright years before the Crash. Here once dwelt the robber barons of Wall Street, and, here now lay the evidence of their greed, a morass of cracked marble that served as a forbidden playground for wild bands of children.

The ruined garden still reappears in my dreams.

My friend Kata, who is a naturalist and basket maker, knows another such place. She grew up in Tiburon, across the bay from San Francisco, in the time when the now-fashionable community was a mere railroad town. Above her house, the high grassy hills of the north coast swept up to the sky, and here in her childhood she and her girl gang made grass huts in the hollows and gathered wildflowers: sticky monkey, lupine, poppies, and blue-eyed grass.

One day there, alone on the peak of a hill under the vast sky, she saw an immense bird sweeping over the ridge, almost knocking her from her feet. It was not until Kata grew up that she realized it was probably a California condor. She still talks about the event.

Teale writes that he himself held a recollection of such a place.

He had been taken by his grandfather one snowy late autumn day to gather firewood. After a long horse-drawn sleigh ride through the empty landscape of fields and cut forest, the two of them came to an enchanted wood of oak, beech, hickory, ash, and sycamore. Here, while his grandfather loaded the cut wood, Teale, who was all of six years old at the time, wandered off down the vast hallways of the forest trees. An unidentifiable vaguely eerie atmosphere enveloped the dark forest; shrieks and mournful wailings sounded out in the empty landscape as the wind blew through the high branches. He was terrified, but enthralled, and carried on down the forested aisles, periodically returning to reassure himself that his grandfather was still there. He only visited the spot once, but the experience haunted him for years and in his adulthood he went back. He never could find it again.

The list of such experiences that have affected people who work in the field of natural history, or in fact anyone who still has an appreciation for wildness, must be as endless as it is varied-forested glens, solitary streambanks, small trash-littered pockets of urban lots, even, as in one case I know, the wild scrapings of an ailanthus branch on the window of a city apartment building on winter nights. The tragedy is that these semi-mystical childhood epiphanies are threatened in our time and in danger of extinction.

For a variety of reasons, children no longer wander alone or even in small bands out in the half-wild places that are often within walking distance of even the most urbanized environments. Part of the problem of course is technology, the lure of the computer, and video games, not to mention fear on the part of parents, instilled by the instant dissemination in the national news media of heinous crimes and perversions.

Some of the fears may be rational, although wilderness encounters always did have an element of danger. But one has to wonder, without the experience of such unstructured, unsupervised play, from what source will we draw the naturalists of the next generation?

From: *Stray Leaves, Collected Essays of JHM,* 2014

Common Ground

Setting: Notes on a sense of place.

In 1652, John Eliot, the so-called prophet of the Indians, having successfully converted a mixed band of Native Americans to the Christian faith, granted the group a sixteen-square-mile tract of land just northwest of Concord to be called Nashobah Plantation. The Indians set up a village of English-style frame houses; planted their fields in corn, beans, and squash; and, having cut their hair and agreed to wear shoes, settled in to live in the English manner.

Like many of their people, the tribe had no clear concept of ownership of land. Over the millennia in North America, they had evolved a system of land use that was based on rights of use rather than outright ownership. At a yearly council, the leader of the tribe would assign certain portions of a territory to certain family groups for a specific use, such as berry picking or hunting. Sometimes the rights of use would even overlap, so that one family could hunt deer in a given area but not pick the blueberries whereas another family, using the same section, could pick the blueberries but not hunt the deer. It was a good system; the lands were allotted according to the availability of game or fruits and were assigned to ensure sustainability.

But unfortunately, the practice, which had evolved over a period of some 3,000 years, was about to come to an end.

With the outbreak of King Philip's War in 1675, in spite of the Nashobah Indian's Christianity and their allegiance to the English, colonists relocated them to Deer Island in Boston Harbor where many succumbed to starvation. After the war, the people dispersed; only one or two returned to Nashobah; and in 1725, the last known survivor, a woman named Sarah Doublet, sold the remaining 500 acres of land at the core of the plantation to a family from Concord named Jones.

Under the English governance, the tract did not exactly belong to the Jones family. The property was theoretically "owned" by the King of England. Not unlike the Indians, the Jones's had leased the rights of use. But after the American Revolution, the pattern of land control changed yet again, and the 500 acres of the original sixteen-square-mile plantation were divided and sold and owned outright by the various parties in fee simple, as the phrase has it. No strings attached. In theory, the owners could do what they liked with the property-which, until zoning regulations came along in the 1950s—they did.

Fortunately, over 320 years of private ownership the various proprietors proved to be good stewards. They maintained farms and orchards, specializing in apples, Berkshire hogs, and Holstein cows.

By the late 1800s, the whole Nashobah Valley, of which this plot was a part, was devoted mostly to apples. In 1905, more apples were exported from this region than from anywhere else in New England—mostly to Britain.

Then in the late 1950s, just when the farms and the orchards in the Nashobah Valley were beginning to decline, a single owner got ahold of the entire 500-acre plot where the Christian Indian village had been located and began to restore the declining orchards. He grew peaches and introduced new varieties of apples and made use of innovative growing techniques, including methods designed to reduce pesticide use. When he died, in 1986, it was learned that he had written a covenant into his will—the land could only be legally sold for agricultural use.

By the 1990s, there was a new crop sprouting in the Nashoba Valley, this one obliquely related to another sort of apple—i.e., the computer. No buyers were interested in land for farming. But the town had been given the right of first refusal on the property, and, after very little debate at town meeting, the orchard was saved.

As a result of that purchase, this isolated, otherwise unremarkable little tract offers an instructive lesson on the nature of land use. For as many as 3,000 years under Indian management, the tract was basically common land, open to use to anyone in the tribe—with restrictions. During the 150-year control of the English, it was granted by the Crown—with restrictions. Then it was privately held for 300 years. Now it is common land again—also with restrictions.

But whether private or Crown or common, as a result of sound stewardship by three different cultures, the basic ecological structure of the land, the woods, fields, orchards, and lakeshore, has endured.

From: *Sanctuary*

Hurricane Brook

Setting: East Hartland, Connecticut, 1968.

The land at Hurricane Brook never was the forest primeval. It was lived in for ten thousand years, first by hunters, then by the gatherers of plants, then by primitive agriculturalists, and then lastly by the Europeans, who, in their inimical way, chose to remake the place to fit an image of the land they had left behind, some place very like England. That part of the experiment didn't last long, a mere one or two hundred years, which is nothing when you're thinking geologically. After them, the forest came back, and this time no one lived there at all.

The end of the human presence began sometime around 1790, when the first of the hill farms was deserted for the richer fields of New York state and the western frontier. By 1865 there were some nine cellar holes in that section of forest. By 1887 one aging local historian of the community recorded twenty-three.

By good fortune or oversight the loggers failed to cut over an area in the hilly section of the community just west of the town center. They cleared the land to the north and the south for timber and hayfields and then, perhaps because of an abundance of slopes and rushing streams, all of which were interspersed with impenetrable swamps of red maple, they overlooked the west end, as it was called by the locals. By 1900 there were trees in certain sheltered sections of the forest that had been planted or left standing by the town's early settlers. By the 1930s, there were stands of beech and maple that were two hundred and fifty years old, maybe older. There were bobcats on the high granite outcroppings. Barred owls nested in the red maple swamps; eastern coyotes returned, bears occasionally passed through, and, in spring and early summer, the forest was loud with the descending whistle of veeries, the languorous song of red-eyed vireos, and the insistent calling of the ovenbird. The trees grew older, fewer and fewer people came into that quarter of the world, and then, in the 1950s, due to the foresight of a few in the legislature, some eleven thousand acres of land in the area was set aside as a state forest.

In our time, simply to go there feels an honor. There is a green intimacy about the place, a sense of frozen time. Great boles of sentinel maples and beech and hickories stand ever silent throughout the seasons of the year. The leaves change color, dry, and tall; branches clatter in the winter winds; the buds unfurl and the forest leafs out again—but the place itself remains unchanged, undisturbed since the last of the nearby farms failed. Go back at any season, and the trees will still be there, unmoving. You feel sometimes as though they should get up and switch position maybe, simply do something with their ancient lives. But the place is an anchor, an abiding vision of security and refuge in a world characterized in the main by constant, radical, and usually unpleasant change.

From: *Sanctuary*

How the Common Came to Pass

Setting: In the loveliest town of all, where the houses were white and high and the elm trees were green and higher than the houses, where the front yards were wide and pleasant and the back yards were bushy and worth finding out about...where the lawns ended in the orchards and the orchards ended in fields and the fields ended in pastures and the pastures climbed the hill and disappeared over the top toward the wonderful wide sky...
From Stuart Little *by E.B. White*

Stuart Little would have loved the little rural towns between Connecticut and the Canadian border. Back roads in this section of New England still exhibit remnants of the old English version of the town common—a central green, a meeting house or church at one end, and a surround of high white clapboard structures on the other three sides, with pastures and forests beyond. Just the sort of place E.B. White's wandering mouse hero enjoyed.

The vernacular settlement pattern known as the common is—or more accurately was—an excellent model of community conservation of green space, an example of mutually accepted preservation without debate or vote. The common was once a cultural fact of life, it was what you did if you wanted to lay out a village, and it was an ideal that still endures in the American psyche. The image appears everywhere, from Christmas cards to ads touting wholesome family life.

The archetype of this idealized town has its roots deeply planted in English history. In its most basic form, the English village (or *ville* from the Old French) was no more than a collection of houses, barns, and outbuildings surrounded by cultivated fields and pasturelands, with a forest beyond. In the old feudal system the whole of this was under the management of the lord, who was responsible for the safety of his underlings, who had gathered themselves together under his protection to save themselves from the raiding armies of invaders, such as the Vikings or Normans. Small landholders in this system surrendered whatever rights they may have had to the control of the lord in order to protect their croplands, the source of their livelihood.

In a typical feudal holding, some two to three hundred acres around the *ville* would have been cleared from the native forest of beech, ash, and holly. About sixteen to twenty families would be living in the village—all told around 200 people. The system worked communally. The families would have owned a number of plows among them, and they would have had teams of oxen, also shared, to pull the plows. They may have had community fishponds on the local streams, and weirs, and even a water mill. The fields, which began at the forest edge and ran to the border of the village, consisted of one, long, open stretch.

These great open fields were ploughed in strips that were roughly ten times as long as they were wide. The design, known as a furlong—a standard furrow's length (220 yards}—came to pass because of the difficulty in turning a team of oxen. The long strips of arable land were planted to grains, barley, and peas, and were altered on a three-year system of rotation, allowing some strips to lie fallow in any given year. Each family planted and harvested its own crop on a given section of land, although the strip a family cultivated might not be the same piece of land each year. Under this system, fields of different quality would be equitably distributed over a period of time. Unless you were a serf—essentially the equivalent of a slave—you would be guaranteed a certain amount of land. The distribution of these arable lands was decided each year at a meeting known as the annual allotment.

In addition to the great fields, each family would have maintained, close to the house, a small privately cultivated plot for a garden, and a yard for hens and geese and a few fruit trees.

Surrounding the cultivated fields of grain were the pasturelands, where each day the herds of cattle, sheep, and goats were driven out to graze. These lands were also held in common by the village but not divided into lots.

Beyond the pasturelands was the forest, which was held, in effect, by no one. Here the local peasants went to gather nuts and firewood, here they turned out their swine to forage, and here also they hunted rabbits, deer, and boar for their larder. This so-called wasteland, or wilderness, was the dark forest of European myth and folktale. It was the known domain of goblins and witches and hideous imaginary creatures, as well as all-too-real escaped criminals and robbers, such as Robin Hood. It was, in effect, the opposite of the comfortable, managed, public space of the common.

In 1066, William the Conqueror, as Anglophiles will attest, at once altered this primordial village system and refined it to his liking. One of his earliest violations of the traditional Anglo-Saxon structure was to declare the forest his private hunting domain. Locals who were discovered in his greenwood collecting faggots, digging out rabbit warrens, or, worst of all, killing deer—his deer mind you—were severely punished. William's ruthless protection of "his resources" altered the ecological makeup of the forest in those areas where it had been heavily used by the peasants.

In fact, excluding people from the forest may actually have had a beneficial ecological effect, at least around the villages, but it was not good for the local peasantry.

In the time of William, rents for lands were paid in-kind. That is, you supplied a certain quantity of grain to the lord of the ville each year according to the amount of land you were using. You rendered unto the lord a certain amount of work each year, or military service. You applied each year to renew your holding, and the terms of your arrangements were set. Rights of use of land formed a great theoretical pyramid, with the king at the top; the serfs, or cottars, at the bottom; and various tenants and thanes, villeins, earls, and lords in the middle and upper reaches. "From the Crown, all titles flow," as the phrase had it.

All this more or less came to an end about the time that the Pilgrims and Puritans came to North America. By the mid-1600s, the old tenure system requiring payment-in-kind or in personal services had faded. The King granted the lands of the Massachusetts Bay Company under common *socage,* which meant that the rights of use of the land could be paid in rent rather than grains or firewood, or knights' service to the King.

Common socage was actually not an unusual form of payment for land in Kent and also in East Anglia, where many of the Puritans came from and where the feudal system had less of a footing than in other sections of England. Even before this time, peasants in England were able to maintain certain rights under what was known as the allodial system, which had been in practice as far back as the Roman period elsewhere in Europe. This held that no matter who was in control, no matter which king or queen sat on the throne, or who was lord, the peasants could remain on their traditional lands. There were no laws stating this; it was simply a reality, but it was such an enduring one that it has been at the root of the private-property system even into our time. It was from this concept that the idea of the common began to erode.

This idea of holding private property in fee simple, that is to say, as the absolute ownership of a piece of land that can be bought and sold, is actually a fairly recent development in legal history. The idea of land as property, something you own, as you would a book or a piece of furniture, did not come into full use until the eighteenth century. Before that, in English law at least, what you bought and sold was land held of someone; you bought the right to live there, or the right to use it. You did not actually own the ground.

By the eighteenth century in Britain, the common rights associated with land-pasturing cattle, for example, or cutting timber or turf, began to give way to a rigid set of regulations based on private outright ownership of property, and the tradition of the common began to fade. This was the same period as the Acts of Enclosure, when some six million acres of commonly held lands—meadows, open fields, and forests—were transferred into private hands by parliamentary approval and were hedged and fenced for private gain.

Here in New England, even though the idea of the commons was still ingrained in the colonial soul, the concept of the private plot, of each man as lord of his own manor, flourished in the wide-open spaces of the New World.

Within a few decades of settlement, in communities such as Plymouth and Sudbury, the great fields and the pasturelands, and even the wild forest beyond, switched from common land to private holding.

Nevertheless, the primordial idea of a public green space, a commonly held tract of land at the heart of the village, has endured. And although sadly diminished, the old town commons can still be found by anyone willing to shun the superhighways and poke around a little on back roads. As one of the characters tells Stuart Little, "a person who is looking for something doesn't travel very fast."

From: *Sanctuary*

Forest Murmurs

Setting: The mythic dark forest.

I was walking home one mid-November evening on a trail that led through a half-lit forest when, for no apparent reason, something stopped me dead in my tracks. There were wraith-like mists curling up from low spots on the wet forest floor, and the air was still and somehow portentous, as if there were some ghostly presence nearby. This is not an uncommon sensation for me, especially in certain sections of the woodlands in these parts, which, according to local legends, are supposed to be haunted. But this feeling was a little different, and after a minute or two I realized what it was. It was the forest itself, the inhuman, dangerous wilderness of the Western mind.

This sensation or belief in the danger of wild places has been with us since the dawn of civilization. For example, just before he began on his epic journey through the nine circles of the Inferno, Dante Alighieri was waylaid in a dark forest where the straightway was lost. Dwelling in this same forest somewhat incongruously—given the fact that the event was played out in thirteenth-century Tuscany—were any number of dangerous, exotic beasts, including a leopard and a lion, and also a wolf.

The fact that a deep and perilous forest would characterize the outskirts of Hell is not illogical, at least not in thirteenth-century Europe. It was here, after all, beneath a great overarching canopy of ancient trees that modern humans first forged the myths, legends, and religions that until fairly recently played such an important part in the human experience. And from the beginning, folktales and legends make it apparent that the relationship between the forest and the peoples who lived in or near it was complicated.

The Sumerian epic of *Gilgamesh*, the first written narrative, which was set down from the stories of a much earlier era, is a case in point. In the epic tale, the hero Gilgamesh befriends a half-man, half-animal being named Enkidu who was a friend to animals and fed with them in a semblance of a paradise. Enkidu was tamed, interestingly enough, by a courtesan from Uruk, who was sent out to have sex with him. After a week of furious lovemaking he was somehow transformed and gained knowledge of the world of human beings. But his former friends, the animals, were now afraid of him.

Enkidu and Gilgamesh, the king of Uruk, became fast friends, and, working together, they set out to do battle with the guardian of the Great Cedar Forest, a terrible monster named Humbaba, who was sent by the god Anu to guard the forest against people. The two friends managed to kill

Humbaba, and then, with the guardian defeated, they proceeded to cut down the entire forest.

And here begineth Western civilization.

By the fifth century BC, Plato was lamenting the loss of the pine forests that formerly covered the mountains of Greece, and there is good evidence that by the time of the Roman Republic most of the native forests of the Italian peninsula, save for a few remote mountain valleys, had been cleared.

But the old legends, and the ancient forest gods and demigods from this earlier forested environment, were alive and well in the clear light of fifth-century Greece. In one myth from early Greek history, a young forest nymph who lived in the wilds of Arcadia was courted by the god Hermes. In due time, she gave birth to the god Pan, who, not unlike Enkidu, was half-animal, half-human. He had the face and upper body of a man but the shaggy legs, hooves, and horns of a goat. According to the legends, Pan's mother was so afraid when she first saw him that she ran away. But Pan grew up to become one of the most entertaining and popular of the Greek and Roman gods and served as a sort of intermediary between wild nature and human settlement. The Lord of the Wood, as he was called, haunted the forested mountain passes above the pastured lands of Arcadia and struck fear into travelers who passed through the valleys and ridges at night. You didn't even have to see him to know he was there, you could feel his presence in the form of "panic."

Pan is the only Greek and Roman god who actually died; all the others merely faded away. At the time of the birth of Christ, or, in some versions of the legend, at the crucifixion, pilgrims traveling in Italy heard a thundering voice echoing through the mountains and valleys, crying out that the Great God Pan was dead. This news was followed by wails of lamentation as all the nymphs and dryads and the fauns and satyrs, and all the old demigods of trees and springs and groves, retreated to the mountain hideaways to bide their time. After that, it is said that the springs fell dry, and the famous oracles no longer prophesied accurately; their keeper, the Lord of the Wood, was dead.

Or was he?

One would think with all my woodland wanderings and my interest in bear spirits and the like that somewhere along the way I would meet some demon or wood spirit in my travels, but in fact, I've encountered such a being only once and that was when I was abroad in an ancient land.

I was staying at a goat farm in the tiny town of Cros in the Cévennes mountains in France, and every day I would pack a tranche of bread, an onion, and a can of sardines and set out to explore. On one of those days, I came upon a ferny ravine with a bubbling stream running through it. It was hot, I had been walking all morning, and so

I settled there, cooled my feet in the chilly waters, and ate my lunch.

Somewhat fatigued from the morning's hike, I found a mossy patch and lay down to rest and, in time, fell half asleep. In my drowsy state, I could hear the languorous babble of the waters, the occasional bursts of wind, and the distant clang of goat bells. Maybe I fell into a deeper sleep, and maybe I dreamed what followed, but I heard the distinct rattle and clatter of loose stones sliding down the rocky scree on the other side of the stream. I opened my eyes and I saw, peering through the brush on the other side of the brook, a hideous bearded face, a shaggy head crowned with the curling horns of a goat and what appeared to be the body of a man. I sat up abruptly, and as I did so, I heard more clearly now the rattle of cascading stones as the goat, or the goat being, fled up the slopes.

This all happened in a matter of seconds, and I sat back stunned and dumbfounded. I was wide awake by that time and, rational being that I am (or am supposed to be) I decided I either dreamed the vision just before I woke or it was a stray billy goat who had come to the brook for a drink.

But the human-like form persisted, in the way in which sharp, clear dreams hang on well into waking hours. This was, after all, the Cévennes, a region rich in Roman ruins, and everywhere I went on my ramblings I would come across evidence of past cultures, reaching all the way back to the Paleolithic era. If Pan were to haunt anywhere on earth, it would be here, in the isolated mountains, ravines and valleys.

Fortunately for the older pagan deities, word of Pan's demise never reached as far north as Germany, France, and Scandinavia, where the forest-dwelling tribes still held sway. Many of the cultural groups in this region traced their origins to a version of the great World Tree, the Yggdrasil of Norse mythology, an immense sacred ash tree from which all life sprang. Most of the pagan gods, both the good ones and the bad ones, were forest beings in these regions; and the priests and ovates of their religions were inclined to make sacrifices to trees to keep the trees and their associated gods happy—or at least to hold them at bay. The Druid cults in particular were known to worship in oak groves and at sacred forest springs. In Greek and Roman mythologies, and also in the forest cultures of the Germanic tribes, the host of wild godlike beings inhabiting the woods and mountains was abundant. The one-eyed Cyclops had their origins in the forest, along with the centaurs, the wild, horse-bodied humans, also goat-footed satyrs, fauns, and silvani, who protected sheep and goat flocks, as well as nymphs and the tree-dwelling dryads, and the sileni, the powerful chiefs of satyrs.

Pan and the sileni were believed to be associates of the Greek god Dionysus, the god of wine and fertility, and would make their presence known in the ecstatic and debauched Dionysian festivals, along with the erotic but murderous women known as the maenads, the followers of Dionysus.

By the fourth century AD, as Christian proselytizers moved northward, converting the conquered tribes, these once-powerful deities began to diminish in the eyes of their former worshipers, although it took a while for them to decline altogether. One of the prime targets of the Christian missionaries was the forested environment where these gods once dwelt. In 725 AD, Saint Boniface, as if in remembrance of Gilgamesh, celebrated the Christian victory over the pagan German woodland tribes by personally cutting down the huge sacred Donar Oak, thus destroying the heart of the old heathen beliefs.

But the old forest spirits did not die easily. In particular Pan, or someone very like him, continued to appear in the night forests beyond the villages. Rather than attempt to deny his existence, the Catholic bishops had the wisdom to transform Pan, however. It was a known fact, they pointed out to the ignorant heathens, that the enemy of God, the Devil himself, had cloven hooves, a set of goat horns, and a pointy little goat-like beard. Even that strategy didn't work entirely, though. The ancient beliefs were perhaps too deeply engrained in the European psyche to disappear in so short a time. Even into the sixteenth century in rural areas, peasants would leave milk and grains and fruits at the edges of the cultivated fields as offerings to a benign forest-dwelling being known as the Green Man, who was half-human, half-beast. As long as he was fed, the Green Man would help little children and guide lost night travelers out from the dark forests. Ironically, given his pagan roots, the Green Man's image, a full-bearded, Pan-like character who wore a headdress of ivy and fruits, became a popular icon. His likeness can still be seen carved into pews and pillars of medieval and Renaissance churches.

A further irony is that the long aisles of the darkened interiors of the great twelfth-century cathedrals of Europe should so closely resemble an old-growth forest. Rank on rank of straight-trunked pillars soar heavenward in a subdued, raking light into the mysterious canopies of beams, cruxes, and trusses. More to the point is the fact that in more recent eras, the terminology used to describe the beauty of ancient woodlands reverses the metaphor and makes use of the term "cathedral," to describe old growth forests— sometimes officially, as in the Cathedral of the Pines in Rindge, New Hampshire. Even closer to the idea of a cathedral forest is the architect E. Fay Jones's unique Thorncrown Chapel in Eureka Springs, Arkansas, a soaring wooden structure with 425 windows that is thoroughly integrated with the surrounding woodlands.

The American poet William Cullen Bryant more or less summed all this up: "The groves were God's first temples," he wrote.

Fortunately, the fear and loathing of deep forested tracts is, for the most part, now a thing of the past and a new ethic of respect for wild things has emerged. We still cut down trees, of course, but not to banish the mythical beings of ancient wooded tracts—although there are some among us who would argue that we cut them to honor the ancient and enduring god Mammon.

From: Notes for an unpublished essay

The Rose Café

Setting: L'Île-Rousse, Corsica

The year I turned twenty I was living successfully disguised to myself as a student in Paris, not doing very much about anything to advance myself in life and not caring very much whether I did or did not. In early spring that year, suffering from the after-effects of the interminable gray of the Parisian sky, I went down to Nice, where I had lived for a while the summer before. Here, I fell in with an international group of sometime painters and students such as myself who were biding their time in the little warren of streets and squares in the old city on the eastern side of the Baie des Anges.

One of my friends there was an aspiring writer named Armand, who was the child of a local White Russian family that had lived in Nice since the time of the Great War. Armand had a German girlfriend named Inga, and in early April, the three of us made a trip out to Corsica to have a look around.

I had been living in Europe for over a year by then, first in Spain and then in France, on the Riviera. Up in Paris, I was enrolled in an independent study program at the Sorbonne, and most of my friends were either French or part of a loosely associated international group involved in the same course. The fact is, however, we rarely went to class. Education took place in the cafés, in particular in a certain bar near Saint Placide where we gathered each day to argue over literature, art, and politics, as if we knew what we were talking about.

Like many young Americans in Paris in that era, I had in mind that I would somehow be miraculously transformed into a writer. My intention, such as it was, was to escape from my predictable life in the United States and leave everything I knew behind. In some ways the plan was a success. I didn't know a single American in Paris; most of the people I associated with did not speak any English, and I had effectively disappeared into the European student community. But my notebooks remained empty.

Then, in April, I went out to Corsica.

We took the ferry to Calvi, on the north coast, and then drifted eastward along the shore to the town of L'Île-Rousse, where we found a small auberge known as the Rose Café, set on a tiny, red rock island halfway out a long causeway that led to a slightly larger island called Île de la Pietra. The place had a decent restaurant with a terrace overlooking the harbor and a few dusty bed chambers above the dining room. We took rooms and set out on foot to explore the hills of the interior.

The Rose Café was utterly unassuming, a two-story building with a red-tiled roof and two French dormers, a wide stone terrace, a pillared veranda, and an interior dining room with a cool bar in the back. Behind the main building there was a rocky promontory that dropped down to a narrow cove bounded on the north by a small, rocky island that was surmounted by a seventeenth century Genoese watchtower, one of many that were constructed along this section of the coast to keep the multiple invaders at bay. Set in a nook on the southern side of the cove, just behind the restaurant, there was a one-room stone cottage with two small windows.

Since there were people staying in the upper rooms while we were there, I was assigned to the cottage. It had a narrow bed, a rickety table and a candle, and not much else. But it was perched high above the cove, and all night I could hear the surge of the waters below, the dark cry of sea birds, and the ominous howl of the local winds streaming over the mountains and valleys of the interior.

I came to like the setting at the Rose Café and would sometimes forego the daily expeditions of the ever-energetic Armand and his companion and simply spend the day lounging on the terrace of the café, talking to the local people and walking into town in the late afternoon to take a drink at one of the three or four cafés that surrounded the dusty town square with its pillars of old plane trees.

True to form, Armand and Inga grew restless after a few days and decided to move on. I stayed. The pace suited me, I enjoyed the gossip of the people from the town who came out to the café every day to stare at the harbor and spend the night playing cards. I liked them. They seemed to have no ambition other than to live from one day to the next and enjoy whatever small pleasures happened to present themselves. I liked the view across the harbor to the maquis, the wild impenetrable scrublands of the island, scented with a wealth of resinous arbutus, myrtle, rock rose, and clementine. It used to be said that coming in by sea, if the wind was right, you could smell Corsica before could see it. A rich mix of scented herbs. I loved to watch the bright little fishing boats set out each day to fish the nearby banks. I loved the lizards that collected around the terrace lamps at night, and the dawn song of birds from the high ground across the cove from the cottage.

In the end, I fell into a strange, perhaps unhealthy, lethargy at the Rose Café. I would rise early and take a café crème and a fresh-buttered baguette on the terrace above the harbor. Later in the morning, I would slip down to a tiny pebble beach in the cove below my cottage for a morning swim, then a morning nap, then a midday meal of local fish, another nap, another swim, a walk to town for coffee in the square, an apéritif at the bar, dinner, and then a deep dreamless sleep, lulled by the susurration of the sea in the cove below. I would sometimes awake in the mornings there and have to figure out where, exactly, I was, who I was, and what I was doing in this place. I was in a state of suspended animation.

It was a good place. You could easily lose yourself there if you so desired, forget that you ever had a past, or a future for that matter, and simply fall into that idyllic condition the locals called the sweet do-nothing, *la dolce fa' niente*. For hours, for days, finally for weeks, I simply paced through the uneventful days, swimming and sleeping and staring across the harbor to the green slopes of the hills rising up to the jagged snow-covered peaks beyond.

In spite of the languorous nature of the environment, however, in spite of the bright weather and the slow and easy-going pace of the people, there seemed to be some latent story in that place, some powerful, perhaps tragic, history that was not spoken of by anyone, but which seemed to manifest itself in the ironic contrast between the brooding, snow-capped mountains above the harbor, and the light-filled, festive air of the coastal community. I don't think I had ever been in such a loaded, powerful setting before and so I started to write about my time in that place.

From: Notes for a preface for *The Rose
Café: Love and War in Corsica*

Old King Cole

Setting: Englewood, New Jersey, 1950s. Trespassing on private property, an entertainment I learned from my two older brothers, has been a life-long pastime, sometimes with legal complications.

There was an estate at the top of a hill in the town in which I grew up owned by a man we used to call Old King Cole. The house was a vast brownstone structure with spired turrets and a mean-looking iron fence surrounding it, the type of fence with spear-pointed tips. The grounds, which purportedly had been laid out by the firm of Frederick Law Olmsted, were extensive and unmanaged, with two immense copper beech trees framing a briar-strewn entrance, a small orchard just west of the house, a ruined sunken garden with a frog pond, and many species of exotic trees, including, I was later told, a rare Franklinia.

None of these refinements held any sway for my friends and me. There was once money in the community, but in my time, many of the old houses had fallen into disrepair and the older families had become reclusive and eccentric—I remember the story of one old patriarch who was discovered in his carriage house one night declaiming Spenserian stanzas to his brace of donkeys. In this environment, a tradition of rambling freely over property lines had somehow developed, a custom that would be viewed as trespassing in any other community, but which for us seemed a normal way of life. We would set out sometime in the morning, small bands of us, and roam freely through the town, returning to our camps at dusk, like the great heroes of our childhood—Cochise, Sitting Bull, Rain in the Face, and Crazy Horse.

Of all the properties in the community, of all the woodlots, overgrown backyards, gardens, and frog-haunted swimming pools, King Cole's place held the greatest attraction. For one thing there was a deserted carriage house at the back of the grounds to which we had gained access and used as a hideout. But the larger attraction was that, unlike other landholders in the community, Old King Cole did not seem to appreciate trespassers. Periodically he would emerge from the dark interior of his house to reprimand us—a tottering old man with a cane and a palsied hand. One afternoon he surprised two of us and drove us into a walled corner of his sunken garden. Once he had us trapped, he approached, shuffling, his cane raised ominously above his head, and there, amidst the wild briars and ivies, he delivered a resounding lecture on the nature of title. "My property," he intoned. "My holdings. My kingdom. My nation." Then, advancing a few steps, he pointed southward with his cane. "Your property, your nation. Return to your country. Respect lines of demarcation."

It was a good lecture, but it had the wrong effect. Up to that time, I had no concept of the nature of trespass. Forbidden passage consisted of

Old King Cole's land and an even more ominous place in the south of the town, called the Baron's, that was surrounded with a high stucco wall and reportedly guarded by Great Danes. With King Cole's proclamation, the lure of new lands swelled within my heart, offering fresh prospects for adventure and travel. But the one thing that stood out from Cole's diatribe was that the world, which up to that time had seemed to me a wide collective space that invited exploration, was in fact divided and quartered and guarded, and had evolved into a commodity that could be bought and sold and held. Old King Cole had offered us, in effect, the experience that must have confronted the New England Indians—among others—when first faced with the land tenure system of the Western world back in 1620, the overbearing, all-powerful concept of private ownership of land that overwhelmed the whole American continent and successfully evicted the native use of common land. Why was it that even in his last, clouded years Mr. Cole remembered so clearly the laws of title? More to the point, how did it come to pass that King Cole and his stock could legally surround a patch of wild earth with a spiked fence and drive out intruders? The answer to that question, as with many such grand quests, I found in my own territory.

From: *Trespassing,* 1996

Prospect Hill

Setting: The first of several different treks from Westford to Concord, Massachusetts, by dead reckoning, through woods fields and private properties. This one accompanied by two friends, Barkley and Kata.

Just before he set out on his journey to the nether-world, the great pilgrim Dante Alighieri had to pass through a lion-haunted forest where the straight way was lost. Here in twentieth-century America, there is a gloomy forest of hemlocks just below the summit of Prospect Hill in Westford, Massachusetts. As we descend this fertile slope, the great pilgrim Barkley Mason begins quoting from the Inferno. He touches his breast and, with a grand sweep, spreads his right arm toward the dark wood below us. "Nel mezzo del cammin di nostra vita mi ritrovai nella selva oscura—" he declaims, quoting Dante.

Kata is used to Barkley's posturing; she interrupts to ask me something about a mutual friend, and in this manner, we three enter the dark forest and begin our journey.

Today is October 10, five hundred and two years after Christopher Columbus landed on these shores with a company of men and arms. We are standing on a height rising above the central highlands of the eastern seaboard of North America. To the north and west, hills rise and fall to the distant

Monadnocks, which give way to the Berkshire Hills, the Alleghenies, the Great Plains, and the Rockies. East of where we stand the world drops seaward through swamps, streams, and marshes, intercut with wooded ridges. This is the known world, the visible land where we will live or die, but all we can see of it from our prospect are trees—a landscape barred with limbs—a stone wall meandering across the top of the hill, rank clumps of grass, sarsaparilla, low-bush blueberry, the blackened, remnant stems of Canada mayflower, brightly streaked red maples, hickories, green oaks, a stately white pine here and there, and below us, like a bad thought, the dark, impenetrable forest of hemlocks.

Our intent is to descend from the ridge of Prospect and Blakes Hills, cross the chain of ponds and swamps that make up the headwaters of Vine Brook, and then follow the high ground between the swamps of Nonset, Butter and Nashoba Brooks. East of the low ridge beyond Nashoba we will follow the marshes of Spencer Brook and eventually enter into the forest of the so-called Estabrook Country, a hilly tract of old-growth trees that was generally avoided by the local Indian tribes and was deserted by the European settlers as early as 1830. From Estabrook it is an easy walk over the North Bridge, through Concord, and through backyards to the Author's Ridge in Sleepy Hollow Cemetery, where we will pay homage to the incomparable chronicler of this region, Henry Thoreau. From there, if we still count ourselves among the living, we will repair to the Colonial Inn in the center of town to lift a glass or two of hot rum toddy and reward ourselves with a full meal.

That is our general course, but given the digressive nature of my traveling companions, nothing is certain on this walk. Already, not more than twenty yards into our venture, we are distracted. Somewhere in the hemlocks below us, a great gabbling of crows breaks out, like an angry courtroom. They keep up a constant yammering and then periodically burst into a loud clamor and move through the tangle of dark limbs.

"They've got an owl," Barkley says and walks off deliberately to the southwest, the wrong direction. The cawing increases again, and the black horde rises, turns, and swings our way. Barkley raises his glass and watches as a dull, heavy-bodied bird flies by indifferently, followed by the vanguard of the crow pack.

C. Barkley Mason III is in his heaven at such times. The little blackpoll warblers are on the move today, there is a northwest wind and migrating hawks are spiraling overhead, and everywhere, catbirds and wrens and cardinals and white-throated sparrows are whining and whistling in the shrubbery. Between Barkley's tendency to stop for birds and Kata's tendency to slow to a near stop when she talks, I wonder whether we will complete this expedition by nightfall.

From: *Walking towards Walden*, 1995

The Peace of Wild Things

Setting: A bank above Beaver Brook, the eastern border of Scratch Flat.

Just before dawn on Christmas morning I went down to my place beside the brook to watch the day unfold. It was a day not unlike other days that I visit the place, except that it was the official beginning of the winter season. The sky was cloudy, and the air was filled with that close, watery scent of coming snow. I went out anyway and rather than follow the cart track that leads through the woods to the stream, I took a shortcut and clambered through the undergrowth that now covers what were once the hayfields that rolled down to the brook in a series of terraces.

Down at the brook the grass on the bank was still snow-free. I sat cross-legged above the waters and waited for sunrise. There was nothing to wait for in point of fact; this day was characterized by that flat, seamless pall of sky that prefigures snow. A few flakes began drifting down as I watched, followed by a few more flakes and then by a steady, but light fall. As I waited, a pale faded image of the white winter sun, much filtered through the mists and drifting flakes, showed itself—a silvery coin behind the black branches of the trees. It was an odd, somehow portentous sunrise, the type of light into which the native shamans and Puritan ministers of these parts might read dark omens.

Among Christian cultures, Christmas marks the day when it is believed that the savior of the world was born, the prince of peace who would mark the start of a golden age. But in fact, shortly before the historical birth of Christ the same date was celebrated by a popular Roman cult whose chief luminary was Mithra, who was not exactly a god, but a representative of the true and only god—the Sun. Long before that, by a thousand years or more, the day was celebrated as a solstice festival. This was, for all the cultures of the world, an absolutely critical holiday. In earlier times, before the advent of organized religions, the ancients watched the fading light and shortening days with dread. It was not clear that the sun would not carry on in its decline and never return. To halt this process, shamans and holy men and later priests, would carry out certain rituals, most of them involving fire—the thought being that the fiery sun would be nourished by earthly light.

In ancient Egypt, pharaohs, who were considered the earthly embodiment of the sun, used to perambulate the temple walls to encourage the real sun in its daily course. Each year at Rhodes, the ancient Greeks would drive a chariot and four horses into the sea to refresh the worn-out team of Helios, who drove the chariot of the sun across the sky by day and sank in the western seas at dusk.

Some of the local Native American tribes would shoot fiery arrows into the night sky at this time of year.

Here, in the silence of the drifting snow, and the quiet flow of black waters below the stream bank where I was sitting, you would know nothing of this. On mornings like this, the peace of wild things descends, time stalls out, and even runs backwards on certain days, so that I might be sitting here 300 years ago, when the tractable old Pawtucket man named Tom Doublet tended his fish at this spot.

From: "Whole Terrain," 2021

(See also, page 111)

Lost in the Stars

Setting: Centreville, Maryland. Nights on a family farm on Reed's Creek.

On warm summer nights when the smell of the river marshes below the house would fill the air and dusk had long since faded out, we would sit on the front porch, watching the fireflies flashing in the hayfields to the west. My family—uncles, aunties, distant cousins, friends of cousins, cousins of friends of cousins—would sit and rock and talk about crops and dogs, horses, and hot weather. The air was thick then, and summer had its grip on us, and sometimes, it seemed to me, the very house would lift from its foundation at these hours and float suspended above the drying grasses and the fields to the north where the corn rustled in the evening wind.

On nights such as this, as the fireflies ascended, my old father would often reminisce about his years in the Orient, and as winking stars of light rose in the fields below us he would retell yet again the old Japanese folktale of Princess Firefly and recount stories of the traditional firefly festivals that took place all over Japan in his time.

I was lost in the mystery of all this and would be swept into some vague, almost timeless suspension of disbelief. It all seemed so real, even though my father was telling the story of a firefly that was in fact a princess in a kingdom inhabited by insects. I was too young to know it was not true.

And often on those hot nights, as children have done for thousands of years, my cousins and I would descend from the porch with kitchen jars and sweep the grasses, catching the flashers and carrying them around in the jars like mystic lanterns.

Timing seemed everything to me, even then. Why did the fireflies flash at certain intervals? Why did they quit flashing periodically, and why did some of them never take to the air and perch low in the grasses, emitting a long, sustained light?

It was only later that I learned that there was a dark side to the luminous display taking place in the fields below the house, and that all the bright poetic legends and folktales had an element of truth. Out there in the real world of the grassroot jungle, the lights that so inspired the folktales and festivals were in fact all about sex and death.

Fireflies flash to attract mates, and it is for the most part the males that we see on summer nights. Shortly after they reach adulthood, usually around late June in New England, as dusk falls, the males launch themselves in the air and patrol to-and-fro across open areas, flashing a semaphoric signal to female fireflies, who lie below, watching. There are as many as thirty different species of firefly in New England, and the males of each species have a set pattern of flashes, which the female can recognize.

Below in the grasses, females spotting a potential mate light up with a sustained flash. The male blazes back, the female lights up again, and, after a series of exchanges, the male descends to locate his mate. Sometimes more than one suitor will fly down and the firefly princess will be surrounded by a company of suitors, each flashing handsome signals. But fireflies, it appears, are discreet denizens of this untamed complex world. Once the couple has found each other the lights go out and they mate.

All is not love in the world of fireflies, however; there is also the question of sustenance. There is one species of firefly that makes use of the flashing repertoire of males to attain a meal. These carnivorous femmes fatales lie low in the grass and watch for the signals of other species of males flashing above. They imitate the flash pattern, and thereby draw the unsuspecting male down to his demise.

But all that is science. When you are ten years old, and it is night, and the sparking stars of fireflies drift over the hay fields, and the wind is in the corn, it is all a half-lit poetic mystery.

From: *Sanctuary*

(See also, page 279)

Field Sketches

Settings: Random notes from all over the place.

In the first image we see only the black hills under a gibbous moon; bark of coyotes from the woods beyond the field where we are camped. Under the star-pierced curtain of night, with the Lion rising in the east, the conversation is of origins; of galaxies wheeling, stars born and stars dying somewhere out in that endless sea of space and we, here, alone in a field on the North American continent but a match snap of light.

A silence. Then the yelp of coyote. Then a moaning owl, and then we hear, but cannot see, in the black above, somewhere west of the moon and east of the sun, a high, faint calling of an invisible company of sky gods crossing in the night:

Shorebirds flying north to Baffin.

In this one an aquamarine sea beyond. The heavy break of surf on sand. A thud, and then a spear of rushing spume spills up the incline.

Ahead of the surge, a company of tin soldiers retreats on mechanical legs all blurred by dash. They slow and turn, and as the pitch recedes they counter-charge, chase the swell seaward. Hobbyhorse heads bobbing.

Another thud. Another sea-charge. And then the jump of flight.

Here a lone silhouette courses over the marshes and then drops down to the flats and begins to feed. It's hot, a salty breeze coming in off the bay, carrying with it the smell of spartina and mud and a whiff of open sea. An east wind blowing. The rise and fall of restless flocks. One of them vaults from the mass and sweeps off on the wind and we hear a triple-note descending call.

In the image you see a glimpse of yellow legs.

In this one the leftovers of summer still linger in the sand; the marshes are quiet, empty, a bleached shell here, a weathered-out buoy, a stray feather. Far off, we see a low cloud of windy gray smoke, then a flashing white signal. The cloud twists, signals white, bunches itself, spreads out, turns, flashes, wheels, sweeps downward, rises, drops, lands in the salt pannes.

At the water's edge, a single plume of down spirits off.

And a wind blowing.

A bitter chill in this one, flecks of snow melting on the page. Ice on the rocks and a flying mane of salt spray, ripped landward in the wind, a raw east wind, a merciless wind, chilled by two thousand miles of winter sea.

On the gray rocks below are four rounded shapes, the color of purple stone, washed with raking oceanic light.

Another wave, another horse mane of spray, a wing stretches, a shift among the forms, another surge, the sound of dripping, of seawater in recession.

A bird head rises, and then, under the pall of a lowering North Atlantic sky:

Flight.

A bee, a rose, a summer afternoon. Sometimes on summer nights: smell of the celery fields beyond the barn. The air was thick then, and summer had its grip on us, and sometimes, the very house would lift from its foundation and float suspended above the fields.

February 2nd, Bitter chill—"The owl for all its feathers was a'chill."

Frozen grass.

A Kingdom of ice and snow. Something howling in the forest.

White moon.

Hunter's moon, dog moon.

Owl call.

Moist earth, grass, faint scent of flowers. A whisper of breeze, poplar leaves fluttering, a spring azure butterfly. Summer soon.

Rising   heat, shimmering fields. Rain,   Rose bloom-   Summer afternoons in a green shade
Fairy rings on a green lawn. They danced there last night.

She too danced at dusk, long hair unbound, skirts flying in the green light.
Wind in the west. Still no rain.

From: Notes—Scratch Flat

A Certain Slant of Light

Setting: East Hartland, Connecticut

Each December, about the time that the last of the milkweed pods cracks in the old fields across from my house, I begin to see redpolls in the aspen groves around here. I know then that sometime during that same week the last phoebes will leave, and I'll see a few lingering thrushes, and the sad little flights of sparrow flocks will become increasingly evident.

It is also about that same time of year that I begin to notice a silvery, raking light spearing through the bare limbs of the large trees in the older sections of the town. The grass will still be green on lawns, the privet hedges will still hold their leaves, and, in the woods, the oaks and the beeches will cling desperately to the last remnants of a forgotten summer.

For years I used to keep a record of little events of this sort. I would begin in late winter and follow the slow opening of the season through spring and into summer, and on into fall and winter, and then back to early spring. Each year, around the middle of June, after the indigo buntings and the kingbirds arrived, the entries would become sporadic. I would record a few flowerings of the field wildflowers, the first calling of the bullfrogs from the pond below my house, but then by midsummer the journals would dry up altogether only to begin again in autumn, about the time that the monarch butterflies would appear and the little migratory hummingbirds would start to show up in my flower gardens After that, I would record the changing leaves, the last of the oaks, then another slump, then the first ice, then the first snow, the appearance of Orion, and the coming of the juncos and the winter finches.

For three or four years I kept at it, and each year I began to fill in a little more so that the blank periods would take shape as well. And then I began to get interested in endings as well as beginnings. When did the last dandelion bloom? When did the snowy tree crickets stop chirping? When did the meadow crickets give up? (Surprisingly late in November it turned out.) Finally, three or four years after I filled out the whole year, I began to notice an interesting phenomenon. Every year the same events would occur on almost exactly the same date.

After a while I stopped keeping records. Almost incidentally, without trying, I found I had committed the year to memory. I threw away the calendars and began marking time by nature, so that when I first saw the phoebe on my land in spring I would know it was March 27. The forsythia would bloom, the grass would turn green, and I would know that it was April 10. The wild plums would bloom on April 22. The first lightning bugs would appear in the meadow behind my house on July 9. By August 27 the nighthawks would appear in the evening sky and so on throughout the summer and fall until the fifth of December.

Toward late afternoon on that day, somewhere between Lincoln, where I work, and Littleton, where I live, I would notice that the shadows cast by the old oak trees had lengthened dramatically, and I would see in the west that peculiar slant of silvery light, and I would know that the dreaded month had finally arrived, with all its baggage of endings, its hope, its innuendos of things to come, and its remembrances of things gone by.

There should be nothing unusual in all this. It is the way people have marked time for the better part of human history. But in an age in which the great circle of the year is cut into snippets, in which response is measured in nanoseconds and time itself has been analyzed into nothingness, natural time seems barbarically inaccurate and, for this very reason, worth reviving.

From: *The New York Times* Op Ed

Night Life

Setting: Scratch Flat

Almost every day for more than twenty years now I have been going down to a bank above a slow stream where the bittern and the heron stalk the marshy reeds and otters slip through shadowy waters. I go in spring, when the stream is in full flood and the cries of red-winged blackbirds fill the air. I'm there in summer, when the forget-me-nots bloom and turtles bask along the banks. I come in autumn, when the marshes turn lion brown and flights of ducks crisscross the open sky. But, ironically, the best season to know the life along the stream is winter.

A few years ago on Christmas morning, long before anyone was up at home, I went down to my place beside the brook just before dawn. It was a day not unlike any of the 364 other days that I visit the place, except that this was the official beginning of winter and it had snowed the night before, leaving a light dusting that covered the ground and a clean blank slate whereon was written the stories of the night.

All the way down to the brook along an old cart road that leads from my house, I followed the tracks of a red fox that had apparently set out for its appointments of the night from the brushy field to the north. I noticed at one point that it stopped to investigate the signs (some of them invisible to me) left by other sojourners out on their various forays. At one point I noted that the fox halted to consider the footprints of another mammal before moving on—the round tracks of my own cat, who slept all day by the woodstove and then by night reverted to his primordial state and set out on night work of his own.

About halfway down to the brook, two coyotes came out of the swamps to the south and nosed the tracks of the fox, and then moved on. (I noticed that they later circled around and ended up at the same place both the fox and I were headed—the stream bank.)

Three deer crossed the cartway about a hundred yards back from the banks, and everywhere in the surrounding woods I could see the little bastings of white-footed mouse tracks, stitching the trees together. At a gap in one of the old stone walls that line the road, a fisher had crossed and headed up the hill; next squirrels, more mice, the double print of a grouse wing (I think), a raccoon, and always along the whole route the fox, trotting at a determined pace and threading the whole tapestry of tracks together.

At various times during the night, most of these creatures—presumably the same ones I had seen in the upland-converged on the stream bank. Here there was a great mélange of comings and goings, snufflings in the snow, scratched stumps, droppings, the scent mound of a beaver, a scattering of seeds from foraging birds, the nipped twigs where rabbits and deer had fed, and a muddy slide where otters had slipped repeatedly into the dark waters. And all the while below the bank, I could see the as-yet-unfrozen black stream running down to its appointment with the sea.

Traditionally, the night that had just passed—the longest night of the year—was considered a dangerous time in the human community. Without the eternal intervention of priests and shamans, one could not be sure the sun would ever cease in its decline and rise again. But out in the wilder, perhaps more sensible, world, it was business as usual, a night like any other, filled with hunting and gathering and testing the territories for enemies, allies, or mates.

From: *Legends of the Common Stream,* 2024

A Patch of Turf

Setting: A wild garden

In 1503, the German engraver and artist Albrecht Dürer painted a watercolor called *The Great Piece of Turf* that details virtually all the plants growing in a small section of earth. This small watercolor is much admired by art critics for its depiction of the visual and poetic beauty contained in wild nature and also for its botanical accuracy. The painting was created outside Vienna—in spring, judging from the plants in flower—but what is interesting from an American point of view is that many of the flowers and grasses shown can be found here in the New World, in New England. In fact, if you look around, you could find the same plants in your own backyard.

There is a small plot of earth on what my mother used to call "my grounds" that I have intentionally allowed to go wild. I have made a haphazard attempt at formality in my overly large garden; but the plot itself, which in some ways is the most interesting section of the garden, is only seventeen feet by eight. On the west side, there is a hedge of crab apples. There are rose of Sharon trees on the south side, a privet hedge to the east, and, on the north, toward the house, a mix of rhododendrons, hollies, and hydrangeas. Most of these I planted myself, but the plants in the patch of earth inside this small garden room came along on their own, and the place has become, quite by accident, my favorite part of the property. Here, on mornings from April through November, I take a cup of coffee and sit in the sun, watching the plants grow.

A few years ago, I made a little stone-lined frog pond in the center of this patch, and running out over the flags surrounding it are cinquefoil, escaped sedums, wild grasses, and ajuga, all mixed in with Siberian iris, daylilies, bee balm, and mints. Beyond these, dandelions, daisies, Queen Anne's lace, plantains, dock, hawkweed, timothy, yarrow, and bindweed—to name but a few—fill in the void, running and rambling every which way and creating in this tiny space a dense thicket of vegetation so rank and so tangled you cannot take a single step without crushing some innocent flowering plant.

After I first put in the frog pond, I brought home a few buckets of water, complete with waterweeds, from the local lake. These in time spread, as I knew they would, but I was surprised to see, one summer afternoon, the darting forms of minnows, probably some species of dace, which I had not purposely imported but whose eggs must have come in with the weeds.

Each year in June, green frogs take up residence in this little pond and sit at the edges all summer long snapping up flies. Also in June, I always see here the hovering, darting forms of robber flies, whose great claim to fame—to folkloric fame, no doubt—is that they can fly backwards. Yellow-legged meadowhawks, twelve-spotted skimmers, and other dragonflies sweep over the patch on hot days. So do a wide array of butterflies, including red admirals, tiger swallowtails, monarchs, and viceroys, and then, in late summer, the gems of the garden move in. Every morning in early September, draping the seed heads and the last of the daisy fleabanes, and the goldenrods and asters, are the lacelike jewels of dew on the webs created by orb weaver spiders, those immense black-and-yellow weavers that only stand and wait.

All summer long the overlooked life of this patch of earth, this mere slice of planet, ebbs and flows; here today in abundance; gone tomorrow into earth or air or parts south. The end of all this flowering begins with the goldenrods, and then the asters, and then there comes a sad November browning, and, by the end of the month, I haul my chair indoors and wait for the first snows, confident that without the addition of fertilizer or lime, or the work of weeding or clipping, or any other of the endless chores that make up the work of gardening, if I just wait long enough, in time, all this splendor in the grass will come again.

From: *Sanctuary*

A Voice Crying in the Wilderness

Setting; A history of the concept of wilderness. Whatever happened to the empty spaces, where one could be alone in the midst of the land.

The idea of wilderness, of a place apart, is one of the most ancient concepts of human culture. It appears in history shortly after the development of agriculture, and by the time of Sumer had evolved into one of the distinguishing features of what we have come to call civilization. By the time of the Old Testament, wilderness was characterized as a barren, desert place, separated from humanity and suited only for wild beasts. Biblical prophets from Moses and Elijah to John the Baptist and Jesus would go apart into the wilderness to reconnect with the wellsprings of the universe. In these wild, desert places, among the beasts and empty land, and free from human companionship, they would find solace and spiritual renewal.

The wilderness idea endured through the Greco-Roman era and persisted, even thrived, in Medieval Europe. Monks and mystics would commonly desert the cities and towns to live in the wilds, and whenever they were troubled, or wanted to expiate some sin, heroic Arthurian knights often took to the greenwood, there to spend their days living alone, dressed in green ivy, until some event or epiphany would draw them back into the human community.

Traditionally, here in America, the wilderness was seen as a place that must be conquered—as it seems to be at the beginning of all civilizations. The great deserts and mountains of the American continent were obstacles that had to be overcome in the westward course of empire. It took brawny men and enduring women to cross the Great Plains and Rockies, and the journey consisted in defeating the natural world—wolves, bears, and, most dangerous of all, the races of wild people that inhabited the "wilderness" (a concept, by the way, that was unknown to native Americans).

Once the continent was tamed, American attitudes changed, and wilderness evolved into a place of solace and renewal, so much so that a whole industry of outfitters, trained to take stressed-out urban and suburban people into the remote spots of the world, developed. More recently, a realization has come that it is not necessary to go off to the distant places of the world to find peace. For those who care to explore, there are wild places just beyond the backyards of suburbia that offer similar comfort.

At the core of all these wilderness experiences is the long, abiding silence of the land; the existence of a spot, no matter how small, where one can find a quiet place to think. Unfortunately, in the past few decades, all of these places, from the wild reaches of the mountain passes to the woods of suburbia, have been invaded by a plague of noisy recreational machines.

There is something in the American character that seems to require the presence of a powerful machine in order to interact with nature. Now, in the popular mind, in order to get into wilderness, one needs a four-wheel-drive vehicle, a trail bike, a snowmobile, an ORV, ATV, or any one of the many iterations thereof. Even the pursuit of fish, which according to Isaak Walton is one of the most contemplative of human pastimes, has generated in America a vast array of machines, everything from beach buggies to powerful, high-speed bass boats that carry the fishers to their chosen sites.

A mere glance at the advertisements in the American media demonstrates the phenomenon in full color—a beautiful wild spot, and, in the midst of all that greenery, a machine. Machines blasting through deep forests and ascending mountains, machines fording streams, machines crossing dunes and deserts—in short, machines overcoming the obstacles presented by nature, even if the obstacles are not a hindrance. One ad even went so far as to describe the machine, a four-wheel-drive vehicle—as "all natural." These devices, by their very nature, do not encourage the one passive use of wilderness that civilization established—contemplation. Furthermore, because they are often noisy, they discourage contemplation for anyone within their range. They also quite successfully destroy land, uproot native vegetation, and even threaten a wide range of endangered species, everything from manatees to Plymouth gentians to desert tortoises.

Why has it been necessary to develop these powerful machines now, in an age when nature has been unconditionally vanquished, when one cannot go even into the vast reaches of the Arctic and Antarctic without finding signs of human activity, and when grizzly bears, and wolves, and trackless virgin forests are in danger of extinction? It can only be that, while destructive to the natural world, both physically and through the attitudes they encourage, recreational machines are metaphors. They are the symbols of our power over nature; they evoke atavistic memories of human conquest that date back to the earliest struggles of civilization against the forces of nature.

But in an age in which not only wilderness, but the biological structure of the earth itself, is out of balance, we need a new paradigm. Quite clearly, we have won the battle against nature, and now we need to give up our war machines and make a lasting peace with the world.

From: *Sanctuary*

The Once and Future Orchard

Setting: A defense for an apple orchard threatened by development.

Agriculture practices on the land that is now an apple orchard began about 7,000 years ago when farming ideas from the Miami and Adena cultures of the American mid-west were imported to the people of the Northeast, the Eastern Woodland Indians. Under this system, the local tribes developed the swidden style agricultural system in which land was cleared, often by burning, and then planted with the traditional three sisters of Native farming: corn, beans and squash. This was the system that was practiced in the 1620s when the Pilgrims and Puritans arrived.

Before that, however, and for thousands of years, the Natives were following a land management system that could also be considered agricultural. The Indians would purposefully burn off a section of land and allow nature to recover on its own. As a result, along with the typical assortment of sun-loving trees and shrubs, such as grey birch, white pine and dogwood, blueberries would grow in abundance in the open nutrient-rich soil. Blueberries are a favored food source for both bears and white-tailed deer, species that were used by the people to survive the brutal New England winters. Venison was cut into strips and dried, and then mixed with blueberries and bear fat to create a food source known as pemmican.

Skip forward a few centuries to the late 20th century and an agricultural system similar to the primordial Native American system, known as regenerative agriculture appears on the scene. Regenerative agriculture is a farming system that uses grazing animals and native wildlife to preserve and restore and reverse damaged farmland by improving soils and increasing biodiversity. In one form or another it has been practiced in this country. But the most successful ecological/ agricultural practices are taking place in Europe, notably on the commercial farms of England and Holland.

The concept was developed in reaction to the rampant destruction of the native ecological systems of northern Europe and the British Isles that developed over the last six centuries where agricultural practices caused the extinction and extirpation of most of the aboriginal native species that lived in Europe and the British Isles, including grazing wild cattle and horses, such as the auroch and tarpan horse, both of which were critical in the maintenance of the native ecological systems.

Regenerative agriculture was first introduced in Holland, one of the most densely populated nations on earth. The experiment was created by the Dutch ecologist, Frans Vera, who came up with the idea of using contemporary grazing animals such as Konik ponies, Heck cattle, as well as graylag geese and red deer, to recreate the late Stone Age environment of Europe. This huge twenty-three square mile tract, the Oostvaardersplassen, is part of a polder, a section of low land reclaimed from the sea (as is much of the Netherlands). This project is one of the most successful re-wilding experiments around the world. The restoration, once established, attracted many bird species that were living in the region, but surprisingly, it also attracted some of the birds and mammals that were not thought to still exist in Holland.

There is another large farm of some 3,000 acres in West Sussex, England, that had been in the family for generations and is currently owned by Charlie Burrell and his wife Isabelle Tree. Burrell had inherited the farm, known as the Knepp Estate from his grandparents, but when he took over the farm was already losing money. The soil was heavy with clay and hard to cultivate. The family tried to resuscitate it, but after years of losses, and faced with competition from larger commercial agricultural systems, the owners decided to change course. They sold all their farm equipment to their competitors and allowed most of their farm to return to its natural state.

Suffice to say that the experiment was a great success and the means of achieving that success, as with the Oostvaardersplassen, was unique.

******

Some ecologists and forest historians believe that the introduction of small plots of farmland in the late Neolithic Era actually improved the biodiversity of the original deep forests of Europe and the British Isles. The vast dark continent of tree cover was what is termed "species poor"—the aurochs, wild tarpan horses, and other grazing species were not common in this ecosystem. But as the early agriculturists began opening up meadows and fields, their numbers increased. The success of new system of re-wilding of the Knepp Estate was based on the environment that existed during that period of change from deep forest to small plots open land. Reworking the land back to this state, given all the changes that had taken place—most of them dating from the Victorian Era—would have created a lot of work with bulldozers and heavy machines, so the family decided to let animals do the work. They introduced Exmoor ponies, one of Europe's oldest breed of horse, and a breed that closely resembles the original tarpan horses that roamed the steppes of Eurasia and Britain during the Stone Age. They also brought in Old English longhorn cattle, an ancient breed that closely matched the now extinct aurochs that, until they were killed off in the 17th century, were common in the British Isles. The Tamworth pig replicated the work of the wild boars. The two species of native deer, the roe deer and the fallow deer, were brought in and along with the Tamworth pigs, their numbers increased.

In the years following, other native species of plants, birds, mammals, and insects began to move in, including some species that are rare in the British Isles, such as the Behsteins bat and the dung beetle. With the proper habitat now established, all these species began to increase.

******

No need here to bring up the troubled future we are facing as a result of climate change. But along with protection of existing forests and new tree plantations, biodiverse ecosystems such as the currently abandoned orchard are huge consumers of carbon dioxide. Old apple orchards sequester about ten to twenty tons of carbon dioxide per acre. Furthermore, they are among the most biologically diverse ecosystems, more so than deep forests or open fields.

A variety of species of birds are attracted to such environments, including bluebirds, Savannah sparrows and some increasingly rare bird species such as brown thrashers and threatened species of warblers. They also attract mammals. Browsers such as white-tailed deer help control the undergrowth and feed on the old apples; raccoons, possums, woodchucks, voles, three species of mice and moles survive well in such environments and attract predators such as weasels, bobcats, foxes, owls, and hawks. And the whole ecosystem, year after year, absorbs more carbon dioxide than a commercial farm, or needless to say, a housing development of the sort that is being planned for this site.

To paraphrase the old Beatles song, the best future for this small plot of earth is to "let it be."

From: Letter to the Littleton Board of Selectmen

A Moveable Feast

Setting: Another ramble between Westford and Concord.

Some years ago I set out to see if I could walk from Westford to Concord without ever resorting to paved roads—of which there were many along my intended route.

The plan required a certain amount of what Henry Thoreau used to call cross-lot walking, which in our time we would define more prosaically as trespassing. It also required, at least in my case, a good sense of direction. Lacking such contemporary navigational devices such as a Garmin, GPSMAP, or smartphone, and armed solely with a knowledge of the lay of the land, the position of the sun, and a sadly out-of-date geodetic survey map, I was delightfully lost from time to time, which was part of the idea. I wanted to imagine, as did Mr. Thoreau, the possibility of encountering some remnant of wildness in my own backyard.

This venture took place on Columbus Day, a holiday set aside to celebrate the arrival of the first of many alien invasive animals and plants in this brave new world of the Americas; and as I forged through swamps and thickets, deep forests of hemlock and pine, and uplands of hardwoods, I did in fact encounter many exotic plant species, as well as a number of people of European ancestry and a bird or two of British origin. But I also came across many native plants, and inasmuch as this was autumn and all the leaves were ablaze and the day was bright and the weather warm, it seemed to me at times that I was passing through a veritable Eden of abundance.

Ripeness was all that day. Even before I set out, I noticed a patch of bright red Russula mushrooms, and a little farther along a cluster of oyster mushrooms, a puffball, and a fine stand of coral fungi. Then, not a quarter of a mile onward, having crossed the first of some five or six roads I would traverse that day, I came upon someone's neglected summer garden, all overgrown with the drupes and seeds and berries of various European and Asian species of plants. Thirty yards beyond the garden I came to an immigration story of a different sort—an apple orchard.

Although there was a native crabapple here in North America before the seventeenth century, the Reverend William Blackstone, the first European settler in the place that became Boston, brought a bag of apple seeds with him and planted an orchard on Beacon Hill. The governor of the Boston Puritan colony, John Winthrop, who arrived five years after Blackstone, in 1630, was himself an orchardist back in Suffolk. He took over Blackstone's orchard and brought over his own supply of pips, or apple seeds, as well as honeybees for pollination. These he developed into the Roxbury Russet, the first of the New World apples; and since these modest beginnings American growers have developed several hundred varieties of apple.

On the eastern edge of the orchard, effectively blocking my intended passage, was a thicket of blackberry canes so dense and so impenetrable that I was forced to cast about for a suitable route to the east. In the end, the only way through was a wide clearing covered with another berry-producing plant—poison ivy. But I slogged on.

All along the way as I wove through the landscape I came upon similar thickets of berries and wide patches of poison ivy, as well as old struggling apple trees growing in deep shaded woods of white pine, or maple and hickory. I also crossed over many stone walls and hedgerows festooned with vines and ramblers. Here was the native fox grape, the original species from which Ephraim Wales Bull developed the famous Concord grape in the mid-nineteenth century. Here also was the rambling riverbank grape, known more simply as the frost grape. In the green tangles of Virginia creeper and in the wooded sections, I tramped through stands of shagbark hickory, pignut, beech, and butternut, and sections of woods strewn with the acorns of black oak and red oak. The nuts of all these trees once served as crucial fare for the native people of this country as well as the European colonists.

Like most hunter-gatherer cultures, the Native Americans were skilled at plant identification and use. Somewhere within the town of Acton (I think), I came to a dry hillside covered with blueberry bushes, one of the staples of their diet. The tribes in this region used to practice an early form of game management that involved the shrub. The Indians would burn over certain sections of the forest to encourage berry growth, which would in turn encourage the local populations of the white-tailed deer and black bear, both of which they would hunt. In preparation for winter, the local Indians would make a trail food known as pemmican by mixing blueberries with bear fat and strips of dried venison.

I once knew a man who claimed that with three milk goats and a working knowledge of edible wild plants an individual could live comfortably off the land throughout the year. He happened to live in Arizona, and I doubt that he and his goats could survive a New England winter, but I did come across many wild edible plants on my walk that day: elderberries; five different species of edible mushrooms that I was able to identify, and many more that I couldn't; acorns, which the Indians would boil and dry and grind for flour; and also ubiquitous stands of lamb's quarters, a plant that the Indians would eat as a green in spring and as a ground seed meal in winter. The seeds of this plant are notoriously abundant—as many as

75,000 on a single plant-and are common in local archaeological digs. I also passed isolated stands of American filbert, or hazelnut, a favorite of both mice and men. In some obscure history, I remember reading that the whole army of some ten thousand knights and soldiers of King Henry V, marching toward Agincourt, was sustained for a day or two with the local species of hazelnut.

Somewhere near Butter Brook in Acton—or maybe Concord (nature knows nothing of political boundaries)—I came upon another lesser known staple of both the Indians and the newly arrived Puritans: the groundnut. It may be that there were more groundnuts in the primal forests of New England—old histories describe an abundance of vines of these underground tuberous plants bearing "nuts" as large as small potatoes, and records indicate that along with the tubers of hog peanut, which I also saw all along my route, groundnuts were an important fall crop.

It was not only human fare that I passed during that singular journey. Most of the plants that I encountered served also to feed the local wildlife as well.

From: Notes for *Trespassing,* 1996

Living with Homespun

Setting: New England

In 1965 the Stephen Greene Press published *A Book of Country Things* which is a collection of remembrances of the way life was lived by the grandfather of the narrator, himself an old Vermont Yankee. The book is now in an eighth printing and its popularity still seems to be growing. It is little wonder that the book is so popular. This is an age when remembrances of things past are very much in vogue, particularly country things. But there is more to the book than that. Some of the facts, and certainly some of the anecdotes may be of questionable validity, but no one can dispute the incredible span of time that is involved in the work. *A Book of Country Things* is in the fine tradition of oral history. It was taken down by Barrows Mussey as told to him by Walter Needham—a man who is old enough to have fought in the First World War. It is a record of the life of Needham's grandfather, Leroy L. Bond, a man who was old enough to have fought in the Civil War.

If there is one thing that stands out fairly clearly about Leroy L. Bond in this favorably distorted remembrance, it is the old man's ingenious knack for self-sufficiency.

As Walter Needham points out, he hardly bought anything in his life except perhaps from the blacksmith, and even then he was more inclined to barter than to buy. Everything the old man used came either from the local woods or fields or from resources within the community. In fact, he rarely spent more than one hundred dollars a year.

Given the standard legend of Yankee ingenuity and the supposed self-sufficiency of the American farmer, this fact should hardly be surprising. In actuality, what is surprising is that in 1965 there was still someone around who could remember an individual who was that independent. The fact is the New England farmer never was entirely self-sufficient, and whatever independence he may have had was happily deserted for the lure of manufactured goods and the promise of specialized agriculture.

That is not to say that self-sufficiency was not a part of the American dream. One of the things that helped draw the early immigrants to this country was the hope of gaining an independent livelihood from the abundant natural resources of the continent. But America has what might be termed a love-hate relationship with self-sufficiency. The stark, somewhat puritanical life of the homesteader—that is, the dream of getting your food, shelter and even clothing from your own forty acres—has had a very strong attraction in American history. But so has the mystique of "boughten" goods and the promise of the easy life through industrialization.

In some ways, the conflict between the two extremes of "boughten" goods and self-sufficiency was evident even in the earliest years of settlement, at least symbolically. Not far to the north of Plymouth Plantation, in what is now Quincy, there was a short-lived colony known as Merrymount which was under the charge of a somewhat controversial figure named Thomas Morton. Life at Merrymount sharply contrasted with the stark existence at Plymouth. Morton was a sportsman, a lover of the outdoors, and to him the new continent was a rougher version of Paradise, stocked with game and fish, strong native brew and Indian women. He soon gained popularity with the local Indians and set up a successful trading venture.

To the south, Plymouth was going through some of its worst years. From the start the Pilgrims had depended on a system of regular deliveries from England for their sustenance. For a variety of reasons, early in the history of the colony that lifeline broke down and by the time Morton organized Merrymount in 1622, the Pilgrims were just learning to live off the resources of the new continent and the produce of their own labors. There is perhaps some kind of lesson in human nature in the fact that the two colonies could not exist side-by-side even in the open spaces of the New World.

William Bradford charged in his *History of Plymouth Plantation* that Morton had set up a "schoole of Athisme" at Merrymount. Perhaps more to the point, he had set up a Maypole, and according to Bradford, Morton and his followers spent endless days enjoying themselves, "inviting the Indian women for their consorts, dancing and frisking together... and worse practices!" Needless to say, in the righteous climate that the Pilgrims had hoped to establish in their new life such goings-on could not be tolerated. Bradford sent a troupe of men, led by Miles Standish. Merrymount was invaded. There was a minor confrontation and Morton was captured and eventually deported to England.

One of the minor, but nonetheless critical ideological differences between the two colonies was their attitude towards the land. To the Pilgrims, the New World was a wilderness in the original sense of the word, that is, a wasteland that was not fit for humans. To Morton it was a luxurious version of a royal deer park. Curiously, in a sense, although he was deported and his colony foundered, Morton was vindicated. In the end, the Pilgrims turned to the New World to maintain themselves. Taking their cues from the Indian culture, they set up a communally-oriented agricultural society using a combination of Indian crops and English livestock.

In spite of the fact that the Pilgrims had turned to local resources, neither the communal organization nor the subsistent nature of their agriculture was to last. As early as 1624 they began to reorganize the communal lands into "great lots"—plots of twenty or more acres which were assigned to private families. Agriculture began to flourish under the new system of private ownership— "It made all hands very industrious" according to Bradford— and by 1630, even the public meadows around the village were divided into private lots. By the time the Massachusetts Bay Colony was established Plymouth had become the agricultural center of the region, supplying produce in exchange for the goods of the Puritan tradesmen.

It is ironic that in a region that is particularly noted for independence and self-sufficiency, a system of commercial agriculture should have become established so early. But in some ways, Plymouth was a local phenomenon, or at least something of a harbinger of things to come. Elsewhere in New England, subsistent farming soon established itself and, except for certain areas where the soils were particularly fertile, by the turn of the 19th Century, it was the standard agricultural system in New England.

It was a system which was in part forged by the nature of the rugged landscape in which it was practiced. The average holding of the 19th Century farmer was typically a sloping or steep-hilled lot of approximately one hundred acres. Of these, no more than ten or twelve acres would have been cultivated; the rest would have been woodlot or pasture or all too commonly, swamp. Two to three acres of the cultivated portion would have been in corn which had become the staple of New England farmers ever since Plymouth. Rye was grown for bread and grain. Flax, along with wool, provided the "linsey-woolsey" from which many of the clothes were made, and there would have been a substantial kitchen. Houses, barns and outbuildings were constructed from local stands of oak and pine with friends and neighbors as the work force. Tools and fittings came from the nearby stands of white ash—supplemented by the village blacksmith who more often than not was using locally fired charcoal for fuel and in some cases ingots from local bog iron as a stock. Light baskets were fashioned by the women from grasses and ash splints; barrels, buckets, brooms, shoes and even bowls and trenchers and similar fare were made by local craftsmen who during the growing season doubled as farmers. That is to say, except for a few trades like shopkeeping or preaching the Word, there was no clear breakdown between those who tilled and those who crafted - everybody did a little of everything.

From a modern perspective it would seem that the system that had been established on the small New England farm at the turn of the 19th century was as close to permanent as any economic system could be. And as far as the relationship between the population and the supply of local natural resources, perhaps it was. But that does not account for human nature, especially 19th century American human nature.

In 1792 the American vessel *Columbia* circumnavigated the globe and within a few years New England world trade began to flourish as Salem sea captains brought back undreamed-of luxuries from the Far East. About the same time, in 1790, Samuel Slater set up the first textile mill in the nation on the Blackstone River in Pawtucket, beginning the industrial revolution in America. By 1825 the Erie Canal was opened and the fertile soils of upper New York State began supplying wheat to the small farmers back East who were hard-pressed to raise even rye and corn. What is worse, New England farmers began to follow the good soils West, first to New York, then to Ohio, and then finally to the Midwest and California. There was something very attractive, in other words, about raising a single crop so that rather than produce the necessities of life with the sweat of your own hands, you could get the cash to pay someone else to produce them. What is more, as William Bradford shrewdly noted in 1622, there was something about commercial farming "that made all hands very industrious."

Finally in 1848, as if fate and the course of human events were conspiring to undermine the established New England agricultural system, gold was discovered at Sutter's Mill in California. By 1850, the New England exodus was on in full force.

In spite of these apparent accidents of history, however, in some ways, self-sufficiency was already doomed in the minds of the very persons who were practicing the art. Subsistence farming, no matter how much it may be romanticized, and no matter how attractive a concept, can be pure drudgery, especially to the restless. The fact is, at the turn of the 19th century, the New England homestead was not the isolated island that it is sometimes pictured to be. News got around in spite of the faulty transportation system, and as a result, the wealth brought in from the Orient in the holds of the Salem clipper ships did not go unnoticed even by the farmers in the hinterlands. At the same time, letters and messages from friends and relatives who had made it West came back telling of rich soils and unheard-of crop yields. And on Sundays in the village squares the fruits of labors in the mills began to appear in the form of men and women in tailored clothes and new shoes. Butternut dye and homespun began to take on a certain air, and that air was not one of what came to be known in later years as class.

Coupled with these events were the long New England winters that held the summer farmers indoors, pounding shoe pegs and fashioning trenchers and bowls. It was only logical that in their long confinement they should dream of easier ways of doing things and of the good soils of the Midwest. It was only logical, in other words, that industrialization and a westward migration would come to the subsistence farmers of the region; their minds were already scheming.

So they left. And behind them the hill pastures began growing up in birch and pine and the paint or whitewash on formerly well-tended homes began to peel and fade. Swallows and phoebes moved into rooms once occupied by human families. Walls cracked, the backs of roofs were broken by the weight of winter snows and in time the houses fell into their cellar holes and rotted away. Rural New England, the region that was referred to as the cradle of the nation, had passed out of its childhood.

However, history is in some ways a record of one civilization moving in on top of another. In the ruins of the subsistence farming culture, the new wealth of the industrial nation found a magnificent playground. Rural New England became a summering place for those who during the darker months of the year earned their livelihood managing the mills and working in other trades in cities as far away as New York and Philadelphia. Within a few decades of industrialization the phenomenon of living in one place and playing in another became established.

Central to the enjoyment of rural New England was the existence of the typical New England landscape, at least the typical New England landscape as it was imagined in the minds of the vacationers. Cows knee-deep in ponds, aging barns and quaint village greens were what the summer people expected. What they were looking for, in other words, was the landscape of a farming economy. And partially because of a certain tendency to stubbornness in the New England character, as well as a penchant for social reform, in some places, they managed to find it.

No sooner had the spectre of industrialization raised its head than the reformers began to fault it. Key to their concern was the loss of an agricultural base. Journals and newspapers of the period began to run articles on the virtues of the homestead — the good life on the farm as compared to the hard and sometimes even sinful life that was fostered by the satanic mills of the new industrialization. Even as early as the 1870s much of this proselytizing was pure nostalgia. Those who lived off the land, in fact, those who were the most thoroughly self-sufficient, were more often the first to go. But the fact is some of them, or at least enough of them stayed around so that even in its death throes, New England agriculture began to experience something of a return.

From the earliest settlements there had been unique, successful commercial farming operations in certain areas, such as the wheat and later tobacco and asparagus farming in the Connecticut

River Valley. By the 1870s, similar, although generally less successful, commercial farms began to join them. A whole cornucopia of exotic and supposedly promising crops began to be touted by the agricultural reformers and in some cases by the 19th century version of the con man. There was a period, for example, when farmers began planting mulberry trees because they had been convinced that silkworm farming was going to save the region. This was also the period when the so-called "hen-fever," (chicken farming) began to sweep across New England. On a more successful level it was during this time that sheep and dairy farming became established. In effect, specialization in agriculture began to emerge as farmers began to supply wool for the mills and eggs and dairy products for the burgeoning urban populations that worked them.

And yet side-by-side with these new experiments, or rather, tucked away in the hill towns, the subsistent farmers were still there—white-haired old men who still cut hay with a scythe and whom the tourists came to talk to and later write about in their journals. Vermont, northwestern Connecticut, areas where the rail lines failed to reach, still had pockets of older order, where farmers survived more by wits and ingenuity than the mercy of the land off which they were trying to live. And it is a condition that somehow has endured, so that even now, in the last quarter of the 20th century there are still a few people like Leroy L. Bond and there are still rumors that come out of the Vermont hills of men who drain the water from their car radiators every night in winter because they are too ornery to buy from a store what they can get for free by the labor of their own hands.

The point is that the idea and in some cases the actual practice of self-sufficiency never really died in New England, nor anywhere else in this country for that matter. And there is certainly some kind of message in the fact that when times get hard—that is, when the established economic systems are threatened—the concept has a way of springing back to life. The Depression years furnish examples of this phenomenon. Even as the soils eroded away from the working farms, radicals, intellectuals and in some cases even recently arrived European laborers began to look to the self-sufficient homestead for salvation. Books appeared on the subject and articles in journals. The Hollywood movie producer, King Vidor, came out with a film, *Our Daily Bread*, the story of a self-sufficient communal farming operation. Men like Scott Nearing, the latter-day hero of the back-to-the-land movement, gave up successful careers in businesses to return to the simplicity of the farm. Reformers appeared again. Ralph Borsodi founded the decentralist movement to get people out of the cities and back to the land and even organized an institution called the School of Living to help foster the idea. Among those who thought about such things there was a sense that the established economic system had betrayed them, whereas, the land, if not abused, would provide a constant sustenance.

Given this history, it should not be surprising to note that in our own time there has been a renewed interest in subsistence farming. Journals have appeared, almost daily, books are published which are designed to help the new farmer learn his trade. Ralph Borsodi's School of Living is functioning once more, private and community gardens are blossoming across the nation and there is experimentation and reform in agriculture— much of it directed away from the massive agribusinesses.

There was a feeling a few years ago, perhaps somewhat tempered now, that this was the final time around. In other words, that the changes this time were real and we were entering into a post-industrial age of self-sufficient homesteads and cottage industries. The sense of finality can perhaps be excused. Every age suffers from a sort of historical chauvinism, but the fact is, behind all the economic theories, behind the full scope of history, there is a certain enduring logic in self-sufficiency. Economic systems, large industries, social movements and the like come and go here in the New World. But in other parts of the world, in other cultures, especially in cultures untouched by economic fads, or in those strong enough to resist them, subsistence farms and locally supplied cottage industries have endured for centuries. If at some point in our history we learn to handle the almost impossibly complex problems of world population, it is possible that there is a lesson there for the industrial nations.

From: *The American Years,* The Massachusetts Audubon Society

The Death of Mr. Smith

Just for the record it should be said that Mr. Smith was not the warm, chatty, local shopkeeper who all the people loved. This Mr. Smith was polite, but laconic; he would answer your questions in monosyllables, with typical Yankee reserve. He dressed every day in a houndstooth coat, a pressed white shirt, and an out-of-fashion tie from the 1950s; and he wore steel-rimmed glasses perched at the end of his thin nose.

Nor was the fact that Mr. Smith sold in his little general store anything remarkable: canned food, dry cereals, milk and eggs, and candy; and, in spite of the fact that the town was known for its orchards, dairy, and produce farms, not a single item that was grown locally. The shop was cool, underlit, and had dusty wooden floors worn down by a hundred years of use. Also, it was always open. Every day, even Christmas and Sundays, Mr. Smith was there, with his minimalist greetings and his "thank you very much" and "goodbye." Try as you might, you could not get any gossip from Mr. Smith.

The town in those days seemed to be characterized by eccentric shopkeepers. Across the street from Mr. Smith there was a hardware store that never, at least not in the time that I lived there, opened its doors to the public. Its shelves were lined with dusty screwdrivers, saws, hammers, and various cans of motor oil, glue, and paint. And, if you shaded your eyes and looked in through the plate-glass window, just inside the entrance, in front of the aisles, you could see a new 1950s Penn Yan motorboat, its fresh varnish gleaming in the half-light, its brass fittings polished. The story was that the store had been kept by two brothers. When one of them died, some ten years earlier, the living brother closed the shop and thereafter maintained it just as it had been.

There was a country store in the town that still sold penny candy, and there was an ice cream stand associated with one of the dairy farms that drew people all the way from Boston, some thirty-five miles distant. People came to the town in summer for the ice cream and the corn and pumpkins from five working farm stands. They came in autumn for apples, they came in winter to ski, and they came in spring to look at the flowering orchards and watch the horses pastured there.

Given this diversity of foodstuffs and entertainments, you might think Mr. Smith would have given up years ago. But in fact children regularly stopped in to buy candy from Mr. Smith, and the locals were forever stopping in to get things they had forgotten to pick up at the main grocery store in the town, which kept normal nine to five hours and closed on Sundays. Mr. Smith was the only show in town after hours—nine in the morning to nine at night, behind his counter in his houndstooth coat and his pressed shirt.

All this was forty years ago. Around that time a highway came through the community and rammed through two of the best working farms and an orchard. A couple of new gas stations opened near the interchange, and then one day a sign appeared in the window of Mr. Smith's store: "Closed due to illness."

Not long after that, either from an obituary in the local paper, or maybe just hearsay, I learned that Mr. Smith had died.

The shop closed permanently. The building remained empty for a year or so. Traffic increased on the highway. A chain convenience store came into town, and stayed open from seven to eleven. The grocery store expanded. A chain hardware store opened. Two farm stands closed. Three new banks opened, one of them an international corporation. A multinational computer company constructed a plant in one of the local pear orchards, and then one day a sign for a lawyer's office appeared in the window of Mr. Smith's former store. And nowadays, over in the burying ground on the west side of town, Mr. Smith lies silent in the quiet earth.

From: *Sanctuary*

Handworks

Setting: Scratch Flat

There was never a sound beside the wood but one, And that was my long scythe whispering to the ground.

Robert Frost,
Mowing

For years I lived in an old farmhouse with a backyard that had been overwhelmed by wild grasses, blackberries, and the young shoots of birch and pine. It was a fine tangle, a veritable grass-root jungle, where green frogs and leopard frogs arched ahead of every step and golden orb weaver spiders spun great jewel-sparkled nets each night in August. Tree crickets and bush katydids abounded there; by September you could hardly hear yourself think for the racket they made each night, and every spring the yard flowered with a profusion of black-eyed Susans, daisies, hawkweeds, and Queen Anne's lace.

One summer day in a fit of conformism, I borrowed a high-wheeled mower and cut the whole thing down, leaving behind a swathe of ugly brown stubble and a silent season. I learned my lesson, though, and at the next place I lived, which was also graced with a snarl of weeds and grasses,

I left well enough alone and allowed the jeweled tangle to remain.

Since then, either age, or the onset of an unfashionable appreciation for Western civilization, has given me a different perspective. I have actually come to enjoy the judicious use of a small, manicured lawn. The problem, I decided, was not the lawn, but the dictatorship of machines. So I foreswore power mowers forever.

Maintaining what my eighty-six-year-old mother refers to as "the grounds" with hand tools is no small task. Manual labor in the garden went out of fashion during the 1950s, when the clean, broad sweep of a sterile lawn came into vogue and all native flora and fauna—and anything else that wasn't planted or planned for—was unceremoniously evicted, either with power tools or pesticides and herbicides. It occurred to me that the antidote to this was to return to the higher morality of hand tools, so I began to cut my "lawn" with a scythe, a device that was developed in Sumer about the time when agriculture was invented and whose present form was perfected sometime in the twelfth century.

Scything is a lost art. It's the type of labor we residents of the late twentieth century have come to despise. It's strenuous work; it's very slow; it's inefficient, and, if you desire a smooth green lawn, the scythe is the last tool you would want to use (although I once saw a scyther in the Azores maintaining a close-cropped greensward with one). But the scythe has many advantages and offers many lessons. It teaches you to slow down, it keeps you in shape, and it is among the most humane and ecological of tools.

Rather than slashing a great smooth swathe through the yard, you can choose which plants will be left standing so that, with a little bit of care, you can keep a flowered meadow blooming over a long period of time. Furthermore, the scythe sensitizes you to your surroundings. As you pass up and down the rows, laying down the sweet-scented swathes of long grasses, you feel the summer breezes, you smell fresh-cut vegetation (as opposed to exhaust), you hear bird song, crickets, wind, and the wide silence of the world.

In my case, over the years, as my vision of landscape became more and more refined, I grew weary of the rough, scythe-created plots that I used to so appreciate. In spite of my efforts, I never managed to create the flat sweep of greensward to offset the assemblage of parterres, hedges, allées, weed patches, and perennial and vegetable beds of my backyard. It was then that I discovered another ingenious device—the reel mower. Hand operated, needless to say.

Mine was a gift from my brother, who maintains a collection of them in his backyard. The mower was constructed in Worcester sometime in the 1920s, according to the embossed lettering on its heavy iron frame; and unlike the modern, lightweight, boring aluminum reel mowers, once you got it moving in one direction, it was actually easy to run. In fact, one of the things I have learned about hand tools over the years (axes and handsaws included) is that they are generally less tiring than power tools—no noise, no exhaust, and you don't have to keep working simply because the engine is running—you can stop at will and listen to the indigo buntings while you're mowing the lawn.

Hand tools provide the ecological equivalent of a limiting factor. Unless you have a crew of grounds keepers, there is only so much land an individual can maintain by hand. As a result, the land that I manage has now assumed a humane proportion—a small, close-cropped lawn beyond the back porch, an area that I mow once or twice a year with a scythe, and beyond that a wilder strip of grasses, which I scythe down periodically. Between these grassy areas are the alternatives-flower beds, hedges, allées, a few fruit trees, a vegetable garden, groves of hickory trees, and islands of shrubs.

This is all a garden in progress, mind you, nothing is complete; but then no good garden is ever finished, and handwork is never done.

From: Notes for essays and *The Garden at the End of Time*, 2025

A Cape Cod Calamity

Setting: Barnstable, Massachusetts, 1963: A hard coming they had of it.

It was evening on Route 28. It was also 1963, and fore and aft of us, low-slung Fords and Buicks were steaming by under the influence of hot drivers with close-cropped hair and high-rolled T-shirts, some with cigarette packs tucked in the sleeves. My older brother and I had been making a boat delivery, and we had been offshore for three days straight. My brother, who had wrung more saltwater out of his socks than most people have sailed over, was getting upset. The exhaust and the roadside hamburger stands were getting to him. His car had lost a number of critical parts and was unable to maintain a proper speed, and the drivers of the big Buicks were getting angry. One after another they would charge up behind us, tailgate for an improper period, and then pass. All we were doing was attempting to get to Boston alive.

In exasperation we pulled over. My brother stood sadly by the side of the road, shaking his head.

"What's up?" I asked him.

"Just look," he said. He was staring at one of the roadside stands that were a common element of the landscape in those unfortunate years. It was an ice cream stand that advertised itself with an immense, towering model of a milk bottle, one of the definitive landmarks on that section of Route 28 in those spicy bygone days.

We looked up and down the highway. As far as the eye could see, there were similar, though less ambitious, stands lining the road. Little crowds of dusty Buicks had gathered around them, like cows at a trough.

"What's the matter?" I asked again.

"This has got to be the ugliest spot in all America," he said.

Indeed.

But Cape Cod was a sad land from the beginning; the soil poor, the trees half-stunted, storms forever sweeping landward, tearing up the coast and spraying saltwater across the whole peninsula. It was a hard land. Even the Wampanoags had a hard time there, and to make things worse, after Europeans arrived in their winged ships, the plagues came with them and laid waste to the meager villages.

Perhaps it was prelude. Even William Bradford found the place grim. The world stood before his pilgrims with a weather-beaten face, the whole country full of woods and thickets with a wild and savage hue, "a hideous desolate wilderness filled with wild beasts and wild men, and only the ocean behind them, …a main bar and gulf to separate them from all the civil parts of the world," as Bradford wrote.

"Better than it used to be," I said to my brother. "At least we can eat in winter."

He looked at me as if I were crazy. He is eight years older than I am, and he sometimes reminds me of Captain Ahab. I stared back, as I sometimes would with him, and he quoted *Moby Dick*, as he sometimes would. "Unfix thine eye," he spat, echoing Ahab. "More intolerable than fiend's glarings is a doltish stare."

We drove on. It was indeed ugly. And as it was a Sunday evening in the summer, it was indeed crowded. We got stuck near Buttermilk Bay.

He began to rant again. Three days at sea never did my brother much good.

It only made him worse.

On the other hand, maybe he was right. Two hundred years after William Bradford arrived, the Cape had not fared much better. The scrawny forest of oak and pitch pine and beech had been stripped, the fauna had been extirpated, and the houses were small and roughly built. Henry Thoreau, passing through on a walking tour in 1850, claimed that the residents of Chatham had to use fog for shade instead of trees. He said the farmers were so unfamiliar with trees that they would refer to them by the personal pronoun, "I got him out of the woods," one old farmer told Thoreau. "He doesn't bear well," he said of another.

The people were poor and had bad teeth. They built fences from ships' ribs, scavenged from the wrecks, of which there were many. It used to be said that if all the wrecks that piled up on the back side of the Cape were laid bow to stern, they would make a solid wall from Chatham to Provincetown.

"Things are getting better," I told my brother in 1963.

"Just wait," he said.

From: *Sanctuary*

PART THREE: ALL THE WATERS OF THE WORLD

Closely Watched Waters

Setting: The Concord River. On the advantages of knowing the local waters.

I once knew an eighty-year-old man whose passion was Sung Dynasty vases and whose choice of exercise was kayaking on the Concord River. Over the years he came to know the river intimately; he knew the quiet coves that the wood ducks favored and where to find the best pickerelweed beds. He also knew the location of a submerged stone wall just downstream from the North Bridge.

One quiet summer evening while he was out in his kayak, a high-speed powerboat trailing a huge wake sped by and swamped him. By way of revenge, coupled with an obscene gesture, the old man lured the offending vessel aground on the submerged wall, destroying the engine in the process.

The event is telling. In an age of cyberspace and cigarette boats, one wonders whether the art of knowing the waters, of intimacy with a river, is now the sole province of old people in kayaks and canoes. Time and running water seem inextricably bound, and in order to understand the meaning, to read the metaphors, it is possible that you have to have aged. World literature is filled with examples. Mark Twain wrote *Life on the Mississippi*, his account of the river he knew as a boy, when he was in his fifties. A year later, having got the particulars down, so to speak, he wrote the American classic *Huckleberry Finn*. Joseph Conrad had to retire from the sea before he could assemble *Heart of Darkness* from journal notes he had made years before on the Congo River. Norman Maclean wrote *A River Runs Through It* when he was in his seventies, haunted throughout his life, as he says, by the waters of the Big Blackfoot River, which he had known as a child. Edwin Way Teale saved his long-planned book about the Sudbury River, *A Conscious Stillness*, for the end, and in fact waited too long. He died while he was writing it.

A river, no matter how large or small, is really not any one thing. It is a compilation of waters, and the waters are compilations of lands, of hill brooks, of dells, swamps, upland marshes, forests, bogs, and those mossy little sinks you come across on mountaintops where wood frogs and toads seem to congregate. The essence is not what you see; it lies somewhere in the surrounding hills, between waters and sky, between the narrow summer banks and the wide flooded shores of spring. And the meaning of river, in the larger sense, is obscure at best. You have to have lived through a series of years in one place to know that.

Henry Thoreau, who somehow assumed some of the wisdom of age before he died at forty-four, says if you can know the local waters you can know the universe. He ranked the poor "much abused Concord River" with the great rivers of the world, the Mississippi, the Ganges, the Nile. He saw the river as a constant lure to distant enterprise and adventure, an invitation to explore the interior of continents. Dwellers at headwaters would naturally be inclined to follow the trail of their waters to see the "end of the matter." He was thinking of earthly territory, of course, and the sea, but as always with Thoreau, he was also thinking of the great transcendental metaphors that are embodied in the natural world. "What a piece of wonder a river is," he wrote.

It is the natural conclusion for anyone who takes the idea of river to "the uttermost ends of the earth," as Conrad phrased it. But in the end it may not necessarily be age that allows insight. I once knew a little boy who from an early age had a natural fascination with running water. One day, standing on a bridge above the roaring waters of a brook, he turned and announced to no one in particular, "All the waters of the world come together."

Thoreau would have understood. So would the old people in kayaks and canoes.

From: *Sanctuary*

Night of the Falling Stars

Setting: Tarpaulin Cove, Vineyard Sound, 1965. The apotheosis of my brother Jim.

Long ago, when we lived successfully disguised to ourselves as sailors, my oldest brother and I were hired to deliver a schooner from Maine to Stonington, Connecticut. In point of fact, we were probably too young to be trusted with such work; and since we had no specific date for the actual delivery, rather than make a straight run of the affair, we spent the whole month of August sailing slowly along the coast, poking into little anchorages along the way, stopping often to explore. Toward the middle of the month, having had our fill of salty ports crowded with New York yachts, we came into a small, unpopulated, unhoused cove on one of the Elizabeth Islands and dropped anchor.

That evening we lounged on the afterdeck and watched the night slither in across the moors and low hills to our west. The wind dropped after dark, and the waters of the cove merely riffled against the hull. We could hear frogs and the occasional croak of a night-heron, and then, one by one, from all across the island, whip-poor-wills began to call. It was a hot sultry night, with the tribes of stars floating overhead and our little vessel suspended between the unfathomable depths of black waters below and black skies above.

By this time on our cruise, having been alone for so long, and living as we were under the open skies, my brother began to imagine that we had descended from some lost race of lean bronzed gods, capable of anything. From time to time, in order to prove this fact to visiting sailorettes, my brother had developed the habit of ascending the mainstays, standing on the crosstrees, and then diving headlong from the topmast of the schooner, barely clearing the gunnels in the process. Now, in the close stillness and the flickering heat lightning from the distant shores, he announced that he was going for a swim and began clambering up the mainstay.

I watched as his dark monkeylike form shimmied higher and higher. Just before he reached the crosstrees a shooting star arched out of the black sky over his head and burnt itself out. He gained his foothold and stood upright, steadying himself with one hand on the top-mast. Then he raised his arms above his head and balanced momentarily. Two more stars flared out and disappeared. He crouched slightly, raised himself up, and then, like a gannet, he speared outward and downward.

It was a good dive, one of his best. He seemed to fall in slow-motion, and as his outstretched figure moved across the sky and the black shores, a host of shooting stars, one after the other, dashed out above him. He sailed forward, unbounded, as if he had somehow slipped the chains of gravity, and for a moment it seemed to me that all time was contained between the waters and the stars. He had in fact converted himself into some form of celestial being, one of his lean gods. All around him, as he dove, he trailed stars, a veritable explosion of light. The stars descended with him toward the black depths of the cove, and, when he struck, they followed him into the depths in a great trailing curtain of light, denser now and more brilliant.

It was only when I saw his submerged figure halt, turn, and begin rising again, splaying stars outward with every stroke, that I realized he was spilling off phosphorescent plankton and not celestial bodies.

Later, much later, and in more boring adult hours, I learned that we had lain in that dark harbor at the height of one of the best Perseid meteor showers in decades. Likewise, the stars of the lower depths were caused by bioluminescence resulting from the excitation of cells of tiny dinoflagellates that move within the sun-warmed waters of New England each year in late summer.

But all that, in the end, is mere science, and in those brighter years he and I lived outside of the confines of science and reality—or so we believed.

From: *Sanctuary*

Of Floods and Folklore

Setting: George's Bank. The great floods of mythology were not exactly myths

> *Climate models based on the current rate of increase in greenhouse gases indicate that sea levels will rise at a rate of about two to five times the current rate over the next 100 years from the combined effect of ocean thermal expansion and increased glacier melt.*
> *–National Snow and Ice Data Center*

Once upon a time, a small herd of woolly mammoths crossed over three sharp hills on the North American continent and moved eastward over a long plain covered with heather and crowberry. After some days they came to a high plateau where they remained long enough for one or two of them to have succumbed.

This was a scene that was repeated many times over the millennia. But in time the rains came and the waters rose and the high hills were covered and the waters prevailed upon the earth.

The three hills that once lay one hundred miles from the seacoast endured for thousands of years after the waters rose and even served as landmarks above a snug harbor visited by a European named John Cabot in 1536. These same hills were subsequently leveled by English colonists and now survive, like so many natural landmarks, as a street name only—Tremont Street in this case—in the city now known as Boston.

The woolly mammoth itself is extinct and endures only in images scratched and painted on the cave walls of Périgord and in the folktales of the lost tribes of the North American Indians who once chased them across the dry plains east of Boston.

The waters that covered Georges Bank resulted from the melting of the ice walls of the late great glacier, some 11,000 years ago. We are now living at the end of a post-glacial warming period, a time when, theoretically, the climate should be cooling. But as we know (or at least as most of us know), the world climate is changing and the ice caps at the uttermost ends of the earth are melting and sea levels are rising again.

The record of the last great sea rise is fixed in the geological strata and can be read by scientists. But it is also true that the last great flooding occurred within the era of human consciousness. And, although the events associated with the flood took place in prehistorical times, before the advent of agriculture and the invention of the written word, the record of its coming and going is recorded in the folklore of the world. The story of a massive flood that covers the earth is an element of the folkloric histories of a wide variety of world cultures.

The Aboriginal Australians, members of one of the oldest extant cultures on earth, have any number of flood tales, ranging from the legend of a primordial snake that called for rain and caused the waters of the world to rise, to folktales in which rains fell for a long time until there was no dry land and all the people drowned. The Bahnar, who lived near Cochin in China, have a story in which a vengeful crab caused the sea and rivers to swell until the waters reached the sky. The only survivors were a brother and sister who took one pair each of all the earth's animals with them in a huge chest.

Here in the West, the first written epic, the Sumerian tale of Gilgamesh, set down some 6,000 years ago, has at its core the story of a great flood. The Hebrews told the same story in the narrative of Noah and the Ark, and the Hindu culture recorded the account of a fish who warned Manu, the first human, of the coming of a great deluge and told him to build a ship to save himself and the animals.

And so it goes, down through the ages: rising waters, and a few, ethical, wise human beings who save the world for the future.

The point is there is nothing unnatural or unusual about floods. The problem seems to be that, for all our histories and our record keeping and folklore, people have short memories and tend to settle in floodplains as soon as the waters recede.

Now in our time, with the waters rising again, we continue the practice, trusting in nothing more than suspect technologies to save us from the flood next time.

From: Notes for *Legends of the Common Stream*, 2024

The Whale Road

Settings: Stellwagen Bank. For the Anglo-Saxons, the great, circling world ocean was known as the Whale Road.

This could have been an old story: You go down to the sea, ship aboard an aging vessel with a motley crew, and sail out from an old seaport town to follow the whale.

In fact, it was a new story. We set out to hunt for whales from Long Wharf in Boston, but the purpose of the voyage was to study whales, not kill them, and the final destination was the shoaly waters of Stellwagen Bank and not some distant sea. Furthermore, the crew was made up of college-educated folks who had at least temporarily deserted the normal world and, as the expression has it, had come up through hawseholes to work aboard the *Regina Maris,* one of the last wooden-hulled barkentines still at sea. There were a number of researchers on board; there was a contingent of college students, and there was a journalist with us, an Englishman with bad teeth who dressed in tattersall shirts and pressed slacks.

I had come along to learn something about ctenophores and sand lances, the favorite foods of the humpback whales. We were to be there for a week, undertaking a survey of the humpback population of Stellwagen Bank. But as sometimes happens on these adventures, things fell apart.

Everything began well enough on a Sunday evening at Long Wharf. It was warm, and after dark the old vessel cast off and we motored out through the black islands, threading through the Narrows, past Lovells, and Georges, and on past Graves Light and the shoals of Roaring Bulls. The city lights faded, the moon rose, the breeze freshened, and the crew laid aloft and began the business of setting sail, throwing off gaskets, overhauling the buntlines and clew lines, and hoisting the yards on the foremast.

There was a ring around the moon that night. The snaggletoothed Englishman came out on deck and eyed it for a while. "God bless you, lad," he said. "God bless us everyone. It's a bad moon."

I am not sure what he meant. I think he was drunk.

I had to stand the dogwatch that night, and when I came on deck, the moon had disappeared and I noticed that the wind was hauling around to the east—not a good sign in these parts. By dawn it was raining, and by ten o'clock, when I came out again, the wind was up. The crew had taken in the topgallant and were beginning to shorten sail, and by midmorning, winds were gale force. At the midday meal, the Englishman lifted his fork above his plate, winked, and made a sign of the cross for the benefit of the students. "Northeaster," he said.

This time he was sober.

The purpose of this voyage was to find out what the humpback population of Stellwagen was feeding on that year. But by afternoon, it was too rough to trawl.

There were grim, four-foot seas all around us with their tops ripped off, and white caps as far as the eye could see. Nevertheless, whales were all around us—finbacks and humpbacks, minkes, and Atlantic white-sided dolphins. But by now the students, who were supposed to be taking a census of the humpbacks, were growing too queasy to work. That night at the evening meal, half the contingent failed to show.

The *Regina Maris* was built in Denmark in 1908 and was showing her age. (In fact, that autumn on the way to Bermuda she was dismasted.) In my bunk, amidst the roll and pitch, I could smell salt and mold, and hear the groans and creaks of ancient timbers. Periodically, the poor old vessel would take a real hit. Gear crashed to the decks at these onslaughts, and when I came out to take my watch, trays and food and barrels were strewn around below deck. Many people were still up, their heads on the trestle table in the main saloon, too sick to sleep.

By the second day, it was clear that we were in the teeth of a true-to-form northeaster. Great white-fanged breakers were slamming into the bows sheeting green water up over the foredeck and raking the topsides. Sail had been shortened even more, and the old barkentine was steadily plowing along under her staysails alone. Now almost everyone was sick. Once bright-eyed students were lolling in the gunnels, dull-eyed now and pale. The hardy crew and one or two of the researchers were the only ones able to eat. The English journalist stood bravely upright, alone on the port side of the vessel, bracing himself with one hand on the ratlines.

He looked as pale as the students, but refused to admit it. "Carry on, then," he said, as I passed him on my way below.

I had come here to study whales, but, since in my sometimes-straying youth I had worked on sailing vessels and had a strong stomach, I found myself working again. I helped on deck, and for a while even returned to my lowly original work at sea, that of dishwashing. Not that there was much to do. No one was eating much. By now, the belowdecks were awash with seawater and diesel fuel.

On the third night, I had to do a long stint at the wheel. The swells were worse and waves kept slamming the rudder so hard it was difficult to hold a course. It took two of us to hold the helm, and my mate on that watch was the Englishman. City clothes notwithstanding, it turned out that he had spent some time on the Solent and knew a thing or two about the sea and nasty weather.

Nonetheless, periodically during our watch, he was forced to excuse himself and lean over the rail.

The wind hauled to the northwest the next day. The health of the students improved; research began again and that night the moon was clear and the wind dropped. Just before I turned in, I heard a fresh gush of wind off the starboard bow. It was as if the sea itself had exhaled, a huge outrush, followed by a warm, sickening stench of fish, salt water, and something rotten.

"Whale's taking a breather," a passing crewman said.

This was no ordinary breathing. This was like something out of time, a primordial intake and exhalation, a great living sigh that spoke of storms and tides, cascades, and volcanoes, thousand-year rains, glaciers, melting ice caps, and the whole history of whale life—from their first tentative walk out onto the dry land during the Pliocene; through the twelve-million-year epoch of the Miocene, when they lived as land mammals; and on to that moment when, for reasons known only to themselves, they returned to what the old Anglo-Saxons termed the whale road, the world ocean, the great encircling sea that these fellow mammals call home.

From: *Sanctuary*

The River Road

Setting: The Connecticut River, 1950s. A sentimental journey.

Someday in the early summer, I'm going to dress in a Panama hat, white ducks, and saddle shoes, borrow my brother's 1947 Chevrolet, and drive to Vermont with my wife. She'll wear a cotton shirtwaist dress, white sneakers, and a brimmed straw hat with a blue ribbon. We'll start early, drive on back roads to Brattleboro, then turn north on Route 5 and watch the Connecticut River landscape roll by.

For the next two days, driving slowly, we'll keep the river on our right, and, whenever we come to a likely field at midday, we'll take our straw picnic basket and go down by the shore, eat cold chicken, and lean on our elbows in the afternoon, watching the old river run by and the play of the wind in the trees on the right bank.

Nowadays, the drive from southern Connecticut to the northeast kingdom of Vermont can be accomplished in three to four hours, if you push the speed limit and the traffic is light. But in my time, when my family and I would undertake this same journey, it took three days. Five of us. My father in his summer whites and saddle shoes, my mother in a shirtwaist dress and a straw hat, and the three of us in back, counting cupolas and the round barns of Vermont, waving our arms out the windows in the wind, and asking if we were there yet when we still had two days worth of driving to do.

My father worked as the "doctor" in a boys' camp just north of East Charleston, Vermont. (He wasn't a real doctor, so I don't know how or why he got the job).

Each summer in June, we would roll up the rugs, cover the furniture with sheets, catch the dog, and drive along the river to Vermont.

We would come up the Merritt Parkway, (counting bridges all the way; there were fifty-six as I recall), and as soon as we could, we'd cut over to the Connecticut River and drive up the left bank, staying in big white hotels and listening to the whistle of the night trains switching at White River Junction. The journey marks the best times in my memory—the end of school, the beginning of a long summer, the smell of fresh-cut hay, the smell of the first spruces of the north, the smell of river water, and the view of that rolling Connecticut River landscape, where the sky drops down to the hay fields, and the fields drop down to the river, and the river runs down to the sea.

A few years ago, starting this time at Brattleboro, I began annually recreating this sentimental journey. The thing that first struck me is that it can still be done. You can still spot the vernacular landscape of the river road of the 1940s and early 1950s—the rusting Jenny gas signs, the old decaying round barns with hay spilling out of their lofts, the cow yards, the cupolas, the pastures and fields. And always, sometimes out of sight, sometimes dominating the view, the Connecticut, the Great River, as it used to be called by the Indians, the winding river, the silver light river, the gray light river, blue light river, snaking through the hay fields, curving east, curving west, now wide and slow, now running hard through highlands, collecting tributaries all along the way, and never ceasing in its downslope southbound quest for the mother sea.

From: *Sanctuary*

A Day on Long Pond

Setting: Long Pond, Littleton. A natural history.

Every Fourth of July the great American naturalist Edwin Way Teale used to select a spot near a shed on his farm and spend the whole day there, recording the things that happened in that singular place.

Last summer I decided to do the same thing on a pond I know, not far from my house.

This hundred-acre body of water is somewhat unique among the thousands of ponds in populated sections of New England in that more than two-thirds of its banks are still wild, and town ordinances promulgated in the 1950s have managed to keep powerboats away—thus ensuring a modicum of silence. Once clear of the built-up eastern shore, you are surrounded by wide waters, wooded banks, marshes, and two coves half-covered with lily pads.

On this particular day in late August, I launched myself early in the morning, and, equipped with enough food and drink to supply me for the rest of the day, set out. I began by coasting along the southeastern shore and found myself paddling along a forested wall of oaks and hickories, punctuated by old trees, some of them storm blasted and harboring woodpecker holes and good perches for kingfishers.

I did have a destination in mind for this time of day—a narrow cove that offered shelter, warm morning sun, and a proximity to the shores. Here, I set myself adrift, lay back in the bottom of the canoe, poured a mug of coffee, and settled in to see what I could see and hear what I could hear by doing absolutely nothing.

For an hour or so, nothing did happen.

Then I heard the rattle of a kingfisher. A woodpecker was hammering away periodically back in the woods, and something—a frog probably, or perhaps an acorn from one of the overhanging oaks—plopped into the still waters.

As the day warmed, with a little more paddling, I rounded the point of the first cove and drifted into the second.

Painted turtles were out by then, crowding onto exposed logs and rocks. No snappers that day, even though I knew they were there, having seen a few monsters on other occasions. I've also seen muskrats in this cove, and one afternoon I saw two fawns dashing to-and-fro through the shallows, sending up sprays of white water as they frolicked.

This turned out to be a curiously quiet day as far as pond life is concerned. Also hot, and after another hour or so I paddled out to the center of the lake to see if I could catch a little breeze. Drifting there, alone with the sky and the quiet shores, I began to think about the thousands of ponds that are spread out all across the New England landscape and how they came to be.

Some occur in wide floodplains of rivers as a result of past overflowing. Some are merely temporary vernal pools that, although dense with life in spring, including several species of endangered amphibians, dry up each year by summer. Some ponds have no outlets or inlets and were created by vast blocks of ice left behind by the glacier. In fact, most of the ponds around the region, this one included, were created by the late great glacier.

About 11,000 years ago, as the walls of ice slowly retreated northward, the millions of tons of water originally contained within the ice had to go somewhere and the myriad ponds of New England are the result. This particular pond lies within a surround of low green hills, with a wide marsh at the southwest end and low ground on the northeastern side. The pond was originally part of a vast glacial lake, and as the meltwater receded some of the water was held in place by a range of low hills surrounding the pond after the lake dried up.

The mean depth of the pond is only about eight feet, although I've found here and there deep pockets of fifteen feet or so. Generally, because the pond is shallow, the water warms over the course of the summer months. But even in the heat of August you can dive down into the gloomy depths of these spring-fed holes and still feel the chill of January. It is an alien cold world in these springs, but they are the source of the life of the pond.

The groundwaters of the square-mile watershed feed the pond all summer long so that the water level stays fairly high. Furthermore, careful monitoring of the water quality in recent years-and the dictates of Title 5, which mandates efficient septic systems, plus a town-sponsored program of rain gardens and artificial wetlands on the easterly side, has managed to keep the waters relatively clean. In spite of their small size, ponds of this sort are veritable zoological gardens of life. This pond harbors over six species of so-called game fish, as well as eels and many species of minnows such as dace. It has a wealth of aquatic insects and over twenty-two species of aquatic plants. Flycatchers show up periodically along the shore, as do kingfishers, black ducks, mallards, and spotted sandpipers. I've seen pied-billed grebes here; and cormorants, ospreys, ring-billed gulls in summer; and, of course, herons and the ubiquitous Canada geese. Reptiles and amphibians are common, especially green frogs and bull-frogs, and snappers and painted turtles occur in abundance—also a healthy population of black water snakes. Muskrats are common, periodically otters move through, and for a while there was a beaver colony at the southern end of the pond.

As with all ponds, these higher species are supported by a vast underclass of invertebrates, algae, and protozoa, and the pond also has a population of a unique species of freshwater jellyfish, *Craspedacusta sowerbii,* one of only a half-dozen species of freshwater jellies, or hydromedusae, in the world. They appear each year in late summer.

Geological and natural forces never sleep though. Over the eons since the glacier retreated, this pond has lost depth. Native plant communities that have formed in the shallower coves creep outward from the banks, eventually forming grassy marshland, which at some point supports treed swamps, which in time will evolve into dry land.

Human occupation along the eastern shores has helped speed this process via organic pollution, and global climate change is currently a major part of this evolution.

Changing weather patterns in the region, warmer waters, and the rising tide of the coast, which is at present thirty-five miles away, will no doubt have some effect on this inland pond, and where it will be a century hence is anyone's guess. But for now, on a still, hot, August day, it is a pleasant enough place to waste time, listening for kingfishers and frogs.

By late afternoon I felt the need to cool off and paddled over to a small isolated beach I knew of, dove in, and then sat in the sun for a while, drying off. The shoreline of this pond is where most of the action takes place. Turtle heads would poke up periodically among the lily pads as I sat there; a green frog hopped out of the water, turned, and settled by the water's edge; and a bit later I saw the rippling form of a black watersnake. It approached the shore, swam within two or three yards of the indifferent frog, and slithered into a stand of arrowhead.

A kingfisher arrived, perched on an overhanging branch, and flew off, with its characteristic rapid-fire call. I saw a red-tailed hawk drift over, a ring-billed gull flew across the pond, later a cormorant sped over, and on the opposite shore from the little beach I noticed the stately form of a great blue heron. He suddenly lifted off and cruised over to a better post, emitting his guttural call all along the way.

The lazy summer day drifted on. I fell asleep for a while in one of the coves and when I woke up tree swallows and barn swallows appeared and began darting about, dipping their bills in the still water. I saw a drift of the tiny dime-sized jellyfish float by, and dragonflies and darning needles were flitting everywhere over the lily pads in the late-afternoon heat. Also abroad were fleets of water striders, and under the dark waters I could see back swimmers, and diving beetles, and some hideous dark thing slowly making its way along the bottom, a creeping waterbug maybe.

This turned out to be a quiet summer day, though, and as the shadows lengthened, I slowly paddled back to watch the sun sink below the wooded hills. Frogs began to call as the light grew dimmer; the swallows continued to sweep the still waters of dusk, and gradually a purple glow spread across the horizon.

The world went still; darkness gathered, and, from one of the wooded covers to the south, I heard a single haunting call of a barred owl.

From: Notes for *An Eden of Sorts*

The Forty Degree Miracle

Setting: Vernal pools

Thirty-three degrees: I went down to the shallow pond in the lower meadow again the other day. The sun had melted the edges of the banks, revealing the ruins of winter-snags, dead grasses, the skeletons of loosestrife; but there was still a whitish gray island of ice floating above the black waters at the center of the pond. No frogs calling.

Twenty degrees: This great engine of the season limps ever onward in spite of the worst odds; in spite of iron-bound earth, frozen soil, wind-cracked limbs, upheaved roots, snow, ice, sleet, rain, ice and snow again. As early as February, the first signs of spring appeared—the songs of chickadees, of titmice, and cardinals. By mid-February, a hint of warmth, the memory of odor and unfrozen ground, and, in the sheltered hollows where the sun strikes the south-facing slopes, a mourning cloak butterfly, snow fleas, and the little soldier beetles that hide in the crevices of tree trunks. No sign of frogs.

At night, thirty-five degrees: The maple sap is running. In these parts, the red-winged blackbirds show up at the end of February, usually on the twenty-seventh. A warm wind, a little rain maybe, mist above the melting snow, and then you will hear the familiar double-sinked call and see one or two males, balancing on the branches. A few days later a big flock will come in, and a few days after that the main body of the flight, the handsome sparrowlike females, grackles along with them, black velvet, their bright eyes gleaming with apparently evil intentions. But tonight, save perhaps for the trickle of water, no sound, no frogs.

We wait. A warm rain mixed with sleet. On the wooded hill above the field the trees drip and creak. Mists on the roads, temperature at thirty-six degrees, windless; the snows, which will undoubtedly come again before spring, have melted back from open areas in the meadow, exposing the beaten grasses, the sunken tunnels of meadow mice, and here and there the signatures of disaster—a tuft of fur, a spot of blood, bones, signatures also of life.

Thirty-seven degrees: Woodcocks are in the low ground below the meadow. At dusk you can see them against the pearl gray sky, the fluttered whistle of their wings and their incessant nasal call, like a small, impatient driver. Someday soon, if the sun ever comes out, we will hear wood frogs calling from this area. So far only silence.

Every year I expect tragedy. In this part of the world we live in a sort of temporary state of natural grace, never knowing if this will be the season when the bulldozer arrives. The field below my house has not been hayed in ten years; the silky dogwoods and the birches are taking over; taxes are being paid on unused land. In autumn we dread the appearance of the little yellow surveyors' stakes; in April we dread the backhoe. It's a sign of finality, of death. In the meantime we watch.

Thirty-nine degrees: I sleep with the windows open. I am hoping that something will change while I am asleep and the frogs will wake me—a sound like distant bells, sleigh rides in the mist, the pulse of life So far, for the last ten thousand years, each spring, they have managed to rise up out of the frozen leaf litter of the forest to sing again. There have been no surveyors' stakes this autumn. We have another year of grace.

Donald Culross Peattie says in his book *An Almanac for Moderns* that the Pharaoh listened to the sound of frogs with feelings of discontent and longing; he feared the arrival of plagues.

Peattie feared the cold voice of loveless reproduction that the frogs symbolized, the terrible continuity of protoplasm.

In our time we fear the loss of frogs; we fear ourselves.

A warming trend: The smell of earth, mercury edging toward forty.

Forty-three degrees: A great bank of clouds creeps in from the west, rain; the wood frogs are ecstatic.

At night salamanders appear on woodland roads.

At two or three in the morning, an owl calls. I dreamed I heard a whistle, then realized that the sound was the call of a spring peeper. Others soon join in. The air is warm. I smell damp earth, old mosses, mold, water. Beyond the woods, in the lower meadow, it has come 'round again.

From: *Sanctuary*

The White Eel

Setting: Walden Pond and the Sargasso Sea

Three years ago a friend of mine saw a white eel of near legendary proportions lurking under a snag at the bottom of Walden Pond. The eel was there the following summer, and my friend saw it again last summer, always in the same spot.

Eels, as is now known, are catadromous; that is to say, they breed at sea and spend their adult lives in fresh waters. For both the American and European eel, life begins a thousand miles from Walden in the wide expanses of the Sargasso Sea, a vast region of sargassum weed, located above the deepest abyss in the Atlantic, halfway between Bermuda and the Leeward Islands. The young, newly hatched eels are tiny, nightmarish organisms, ribbonlike, transparent, and equipped with huge, apparently useless teeth. These tiny *leptocephali*, as they are called, are so unlike eels that they were not recognized as such until the mystery of the eel life cycle was unlocked in the early twentieth century.

A year after hatching, the larvae metamorphose into elvers, the small silvery eels that gather in vast schools up and down the coast of North America in March and April. On the proper night, when it is warm and rainy and the tide is rising, they stream en masse to the coast to begin their journey upstream. Eels are very common. There is not a single bay, harbor, stream mouth estuary, tidal marsh, or river from Cape Sable to Cape Cod that does not support at least a small population. And during spring migration they run up virtually every unobstructed stream throughout the Gulf of Maine, forcing their way against currents, slithering over low dams, around, and even over waterfalls, and climbing wet mossy rocks, until they reach the lakes and ponds of the headwaters. They occur in the Connecticut Lakes in Canada and in New Hampshire at the head of the Connecticut River. They are found in the Rangeley Lakes at the head of the Androscoggin and Matagamon Lake at the head of the east branch of the Penobscot, and there are records of eels in apparently landlocked locations as much as eight thousand feet above sea level.

Once established in the upper reaches of the fresh bodies of water, they spend their adult lives fattening themselves, until, after some ten or twenty years, having achieved a length of as much as five feet, they are seized with an urge to return to their primal waters

Then, on rainy autumnal nights, they begin a reverse journey to the sea, down mountain streams, through narrow raceways, down brooks, over dams, to small rivers, to main stem branches. Through estuaries, out into the shallow seas of the continental bank and onward into the dark, open Atlantic, where for all intents and purposes they disappear from view. They no longer feed at this point in their lives. They only swim. For weeks they swim, all through October, through November and December, until finally, in mid-winter, in the waters of the Sargasso Sea, exhausted, nearly expended, the life force withering inside them, they summon their last reserves of energy, spawn, lay their eggs, and die, their role in the great cycle completed.

On rainy autumnal nights, eels have been seen crossing overland in wet meadows. They seem obsessed during their youth with a desire to swim against currents, surmounting all but the highest obstacles. There are documented cases of eels swimming as many as thirty-one miles in conduits and underground rivers. They climb into the foothills and mountains; they swim up water mains and aqueducts; they are even able to reach bodies of water with no apparent inlet or outlet.

Walden Pond is such a body of water. It has no connection with the sea; it is an outpouring of the local water table. The closest body of running water is Fairhaven Bay on the Sudbury River, which is about a mile from Walden, separated by a series of marshy ponds, intervening dry ridges, and railroad tracks. And yet Walden has at least one eel.

There used to be a theory that Walden Pond was spring-fed; that there was a "leach hole" in the bottom of the pond through which the exceptionally clear waters rose and fell, and up which, theoretically, an eel could swim. But the so-called leach hole, rediscovered and analyzed in our time, is merely a one-hundred-and-three-foot depression in Walden Pond, and it has a solid bottom.

In theory, the Walden eel could have been mixed in with the trout that are stocked in the pond each year by the state. But, according to Bill Schold, the manager of Walden Pond State Reservation, that seems unlikely. The most logical explanation is that, as a young elver, the white eel of Walden Pond worked its way up through the marshes and wetlands from the southeastern end of Fairhaven Bay to the Andromeda Ponds, which are separated from Walden by the high, dry embankment of the Fitchburg Line of the MBTA Commuter Railroad.

Some rainy night in late spring, somehow sensing the presence of a large body of water no more than one or two hundred yards away, the white eel climbed out of its native element, crossed the tracks, and skidded down the banks to the waters of Walden, where it remains to this day.

No doubt, some rainy night, perhaps this very autumn, it will reverse the process.

The full story of the life cycle of the eel was not unraveled until 1923, after nearly twenty years of work by the Danish scientist Johannes Schmidt. It is a great pity that the universal proprietor of Walden, Henry Thoreau, could not have known the story. He would have found deep meaning in the eel's journey from cradle to grave. It is a story of metaphorical proportions. It stitches land and sea together; it covers vast distances, remote seas, and summery upland ponds. Furthermore, it is cyclic, symbolic, as Henry might say, of the great karmic circles of life and death recounted in the Vedas.

Those of us who live inland, under the impression that we are far from the ocean and its tides and have no connection to the great forces that drive the sea or the land, or, for that matter, our own lives, would do well to take note of the eels' odyssey. Our voyaging is but a great circle sailing, as Henry pointed out in the last pages of *Walden*.

From: *Sanctuary*

Of Time and the River

Setting: The North River: Long memories of the naturalist William G. Vinal.

For three hundred and fifty years white people have lived on the glacial outwash plains and low hills that border the banks and marshes of the North River. Ninety of those years, that is, approximately one-fourth of the total span of the recorded history of Plymouth County, William G. Vinal, or Cap'n Bill, as he prefers to be called, has either lived, worked, or closely followed the ebb and flow of human events along the river. He was born four miles from its banks in what was once South Scituate but is now Norwell. He was fed on its shellfish, herring and cod, gathered salt hay from its marshes and watched the kaleidoscope of its seasons as they turned from the greys of winter to the warm greens of spring and summer and then back to winter again. He grew up along the river, grew into an adult and left and then grew into old age and returned. As a result, partly through his own design, and partly by accident of time and place, he became so much a part of the North River's history that it is difficult to discuss the one without mentioning the other.

It was 1881 when he was born and life along the North River was in flux. Ten years earlier the last of the famous North River vessels had been built. It was launched from the Chittenden Yard in South Scituate, and as if to solidify the relationship of the Vinals and the river, it was commanded by Cap'n Bill's grandfather. Seventeen years after his birth, in 1898, the Portland Gale managed to accomplish what the dreamers and engineers had failed to do by opening a new mouth between the Third and Fourth Cliffs in Scituate. That storm marked a turning. From then on, the salt haying ceased and the industries that had developed along the tributaries of the river for one reason or another, slipped into poor economic straits and faded. Labor was now cheaper in other areas, steam power was replacing the water power of the North River mills, transportation was better than it had been in the past and slowly, the various industries, and after them whole families, began to filter out of the North River watershed to other areas.

Not that it mattered to Cap'n Bill. Not at that time at least. His early life was spent on his father's farm, and in the proper season, on the river marshes where they went for salt hay. From his house in South Scituate Cap'n Bill was a long way from the river. Four miles in the 1890s is not what four miles is today. So the river was a separate thing, a place where they went only on special occasions. And yet from his South Scituate home he could glimpse the lowering sea-skies that hung over the river mouth in winter, and watch the summer winds build thunderheads above the open marshes. He and his family, in spite of the distance, were still under the sway of the river.

It was the summer season that he loved the best, the long light, the easy days, fishing, and above all, in spite of the hard work and the sweat, salt haying with his father and friends. They would gather at dawn on those days—his father, the boys, the wagon and the horse that would draw them there. They would fill earthen jugs with a cool drink of water, molasses, and ginger known as switchel, pack bread and butter and perhaps cucumbers from the garden and start out. The old man took his time, stopping occasionally to talk with friends, stopping at the local store and finally just before they got to the salt marshes, stopping at the last fresh brook to water the horse and swell the dried out wooden axles.

Like many of the salt hayers of the area, William Vinal still cut hay by hand. He would begin at the high ground and scythe toward the river "down medder" as they would say. Behind him came the boys, raking the scatterings with long-handled rakes known as bull rakes. They would pile the hay into bunches and then jam long hay poles underneath and carry their cargo to the waiting wagon to be carefully stacked for the sweet ride home.

At noon they would stop for lunch, uncover the jug of switchel from the bushel of hay where they had stored it to keep it cool, salt their cucumbers, butter their bread and watch the flights of ducks and shorebirds rise and settle from the uncut marshes in the distance. They would mix their time with work and pleasure so that in the long film of Cap'n Bill's memory, the one has blended with the other. There were easy vistas every time they glanced up from their work, there was the smooth swish of the scythe, the grasses falling evenly behind the blade and the sharp contrast between that which had been cut and stacked and that which had yet to be cut. And there was always the wildlife, the abrupt whistles of the yellowlegs and other shorebirds and the circling pairs of ducks, and all around them like a curving, blue wall, there were the welling skies of the South Shore of Massachusetts.

Yet in spite of these peaceful days of summer and the apparent purity of the seasons, there were tidings of a turn along the river in his time, a prefiguration of the changes that were taking place in the rest of the nation. And ironically, as if progress were turned upside down, the North River was to benefit.

If he had had the mobility, Bill Vinal could have experienced a part of that change. There was a swimming hole in the river at Curtis' Crossing in Hanover. About the time of his birth it was a popular place with the local boys. They swam through their summers there and tread out eels or dug freshwater clams whenever they weren't swimming. By the time Cap'n Bill was ten, that is, just about the time he would have been using it to swim in, it had been fouled by refuse from a rubber mill and no boys came there any more.

The rubber mill was not the only industry along the river. There were tack factories supplying shoe nails for the Brockton shoe manufacturers and upholstery tacks for the nearby furniture makers. There were saw mills, box mills and shingle mills, trunk factories, iron works, mills for leather, woolens and cotton and an assortment of small privately-run home industries. Most of them were water-powered, depending on the head of water artificially created along the slow-running tributaries of the river by use of mill ponds, dams and flash boards. In view of the abundance, it would seem that industry was at some peak of development on the North River. And yet, compared with the rest of New England, things were in a decline.

Industry was nothing new to the river: in fact the North River was the compost for one of the greatest trades ever to flower and fade in that blossoming garden of the New World. It was on the banks of the North River that shipbuilders developed the skills that later produced the clipper ship. And if there is indeed such a thing as a marriage of art and industry, of the functional and the beautiful, then it must have been in the graceful lines of those slim-winged ships.

Between 1645 and 1871 more than one thousand vessels were built along the river. The first was some time-obscured fishing vessel and the last was the *Helen W. Foster*. In between lay the framework and keel of American maritime history. The *Columbia* built at Briggs yard in 1773—the first American vessel to circumnavigate the globe and have the privilege of having another, more grand, but no less important river named after her on the North west coast of America. The whale ship *Essex*—the only known vessel to have gained the somewhat questionable honor of being stove and sunk by a whale. The *Harmony*—sunk also by a whale, although in a different manner. The *Beaver*—one of the three ships in the Boston Tea Party. The *Globe*—the stage for one of the few mutinies in American history. If nothing else there were names—a 225-year list of vessels that provided the vehicles for the trades that made this country the greatest seafaring nation of the period and gave the designers the training for what they would later produce in the famous yards that gave the world the clipper ship.

And all that on the North River, a narrow turning arm of the sea that stretches inland like some rippling sea snake with its head in Cape Cod Bay and its body winding across the land. It was a strange place to build ships. It is less than ten miles as a coot flies from the coast to that arbitrary point at Curtis' Crossing which men have decided marks the beginning of the North River and the end of the Indian Head. But it is twenty or more by water. It was hardly suited to the trade—narrow, looped, and lined with marshes. But the men of those times had a way of making the land fit their needs, and only occasionally fitting their needs to the land. They dug out the banks opposite the yards so that the larger vessels would have turning room when they were launched. They sometimes needed ten or twelve tides to make it down to the sea and they often had to ram or kedge their way over the shallows in the river, and then again over a sand bar off the mouth. They walked their vessels downstream, perched a pilot on the bows and a team of men on each bank and hauled their new-built prize slowly and carefully through the grassy marshland as if she were some oversized canal boat. Near Marshfield they would put into new yards where they would step the masts, set up the standing rigging, reeve the running gear, bend on new sail and set out for the fortunes of 19th Century world trade.

So industry was nothing new to the North River by the time Cap'n Bill was born. But the trades of the late 1800s were not made of the same matter as the earlier works. When the white man first came to the South Shore, the low hills along the North River were coated with veteran white oak, black walnut and white pine. It was that good supply of timber linked with the trade that was beginning to blossom in the Massachusetts Bay Colony to the north that brought shipbuilding to the river. And it was the need for fittings and tools, and the supply of bog iron ore in the nearby swamps and marshes that brought industries like the famous Curtis Iron Works that cast the anchors for the *Constitution* and the smaller mills that were associated with shipbuilding. In other words, there was a food chain of industry, a dependence on the available natural resources of the area. And while the North River may not have been the ideal site in terms of width or the depths of her waters, she made up, in white pine, oak and black walnut what she lacked in topography.

But there is something very basic in that story about the goose that laid the golden egg. It was not long before men exhausted the supply of local timber from the hills and dug out the bog iron ore from the nearby wetlands. They began to build bigger ships, too big for the narrow North River and by the late 1840s the Middlesex Canal had opened the white pine forests of New Hampshire for the East Boston shipyards.

With the diminishing supply of local resources, shipbuilding started to decline. At the same time, the other industries along the river began to diversify, but unlike shipbuilding, they depended on transportation to supply their resources and the slow running tributaries to supply their power. Without the local resources, or the power, or the mother industry to spur them on, the associated industries began a decline and one by one set their flashboards for the last time. Some died by fire, some were washed out by floods and some were swamped by economics.

Had he thought to document it, Cap'n Bill could have seen the industries going. Except for his farming father, his family was now looking to the Clapp shoe factories at Weymouth for work, and he himself was raising ducks and geese as flyers for Edwin Clapp. He was paid not by money, but new shoes, large and shiny and contrasting sharply with the plainness of his everyday clothes.

In November of 1898, one of the worst storms in the recorded history of New England hit the coast. The great steamer *Portland* went down in that storm so they called it the Portland Gale. It is a convenient turning point in the history of the river. After the storm, the new mouth opened at Scituate, the tide levels increased, the salinity of the river changed, cedars died off in the bordering swamps, salt haying dwindled and a few more industries either flooded or failed. It is ironic that for years the ship builders had longed for a new mouth through the barrier beach. Now that the industry was dead, the new mouth appeared, as if to mock the works of man.

There is a ghostly sense of history that pervades the North River that can best be appreciated by standing at the site of one of the former shipyards while the grasshoppers whisper in the late summer grasses and the catbirds whine in the sumac thickets on the banks. There is an eerie sense of the impermanence of human endeavor in the empty expanses where the salt hayers once swung their scythes. There is time in the running waters, and timelessness at the quiet turning of the tides.

I once suggested to Cap'n Bill that it is this almost mystical aura of history that is the essence of the North River. He looked up from the table where we were sitting and said, "Perhaps. But the important thing is to save it for the future." That comment is typical. In the long span of his years, he is a blend of two ages and a catalyst for each. He can reach back along the tapestry of his memory and relive another era on the river when time flowed more gently. And yet while he has earned the right to retire to the comfort of his memory and avoid the chaos of the present, he is equally interested in today, and more especially the future. At ninety-three he is no laggard in current events.

Cap'n Bill keeps a book of newspaper clippings, articles he has written, newsletters concerning the river, names, references and pamphlets. He keeps a close watch on the North River and the sometimes absurd flips of local politics. He harps on the quality of the future, and expounds on the past. But it is a curious twist of destiny that in spite of his concern and interest he may have missed some of the best years for the river.

One year after the Portland Gale Cap'n Bill went away to college and for the next fifty-three years he no longer lived permanently on the river, although he always came back and he always stayed in touch. Those fifty-three years marked an interlude for the river, a relaxation between the explosiveness of the late industrial revolution and the present. While the rest of the nation was forging the mold for the environmental chaos that we now exist in, the North River was slipping into a quiet state of innocence that resembled more closely its earlier days when Wampanoags gathered shellfish from its mud flats.

There is a message of hope in the North River. Those interim years provide a living testimony to the ability of running water to regenerate itself after the onslaught of human activity. Even before the last of the industries had departed, the striped bass returned to the waters. The herring once more forced their way up the tributaries in spring and the vegetation closed in around the abandoned mills. Throughout New England, mills were thrumming with activity and riverine life was dying, but the North River, the mother of them all in a sense, was enjoying a retirement, as if some greater force had granted her a reward for the struggle of giving birth.

As honest or energetic as they may seem, there is no sense in romanticizing the early industries. They exacted a heavy toll in their passage. Sawdust, bark and woodchips clogged the tributaries near the saw mills. Slag heaps from the iron mills spilled into the river and the discarded rubber from the mill at Curtis' Crossing gave off an unbearable stench whenever the river was low. The great forests of oak and black walnut were felled for ships and fuel, and the fluctuating pond levels caused by the manipulation of the flashboards in the mill dams created a watery no-man's-land where only a limited amount of aquatic life could exist. Also, the numerous dams blocked the passage of the anadromous fish that move in from the sea each spring and prevented reproduction. And although communities along the river were conscious of the problem and sometimes required that the mills provide fish ladders, the fish populations dropped.

Even the salt haying had some effect. The salt marshes were a recognized and valued resource before the importation of English hay. Salt marsh grass (*Spartina alterniflora*) was used for thatch, the salt fox grass, spike grass and black grass were used for hay and the eel grass of the shallow waters was banked against the houses as insulation during winter. To mark the ownership of these valuable pastures of the sea, and to encourage faster runoff of tidal waters, ditches were dug through the marshes. Although they may have indirectly benefited marine resources by encouraging the return of the nutrient-rich waters by draining the shallow pannes where the water remained, these ditches decimated the populations of insects and other invertebrates that provided food for the flocks of shorebirds.

The North River is particularly vulnerable to such activity because it is tidal for most of its twenty-mile length, and therefore is slow to flush out any refuse that is spilled into it. As a result, the combined effects of the industries slowly deteriorated the quality of the river so that by the middle of the 19th century it had been entirely altered from its original state. Wildlife was rare, shorebird populations were low, and many species of fish had deserted the waters. Some of the more observant members of the river communities were not entirely ignorant of this, in fact a local historian remarked in 1889, that unless some action was taken, "all fish will become as strangers to the river, as bass and salmon have already."

Just at the point when the river was at its worst, the seeds of a new period were germinating. By the early 1900s it was improving to the extent that most of the people now living remember the North River as a pure stream, although some can recall the great banks of sawdust and the rubber bottom at Curtis' Crossing.

For some fifty years the river reposed in this state of tranquility. Cap'n Bill had gone. He was teaching now, first at Marshall College, then at Syracuse, then Western Reserve University and finally the University of Massachusetts. He was forming theories on outdoor education, starting departments of nature recreation and using techniques and methods which only now, forty years later, are becoming standard for education and land-use planning. He was writing, working, teaching, trying to educate the public to the fact that there is another world just beyond its doors, a history in local streets and streams, and a natural world that sustains us all.

In 1951 he retired as Professor Emeritus from the University of Massachusetts and returned to the river. By now, transportation and communication were better than they had been when he left, and he became more involved with the river than ever. But just beyond the purity of its waters, and the wild tangle of its banks, he saw the potential for a destruction so vast, that it would eclipse the petty sunburst of the industrial past.

By 1948 plans were laid for the construction of a major coastal highway linking Boston to the resorts of Cape Cod. By the early 1950s the plans were being implemented, and by 1968 Route 3 was completed. As if by accident, and with no concern for the environmental after effects, the highway happened to cross the North River. And that spelled an end to the quiescent state between the recent past and today.

There is a reserve of energy behind Cap'n Bill's grey eyes. There is strength or something beyond strength that keeps him active, keeps him angry in spite of the ninety-three winters that he has seen. He has a way about him. A sort of half-smile when he talks, and a quick glance that has the knowledge not only of time and things of the earth, but also the vagaries of human politics. You see that glance often when you talk to him about what Route 3 has done to the North River.

Cap'n Bill's books of clippings make up a history. There is a record of change written there that says something about the speed with which modern man can alter an environment. The problems are not unfamiliar—the buildup of the summer population, the increase in motor boating along the formerly silent waters, the construction of new bridges and roads. And then finally, the turn from a summer colony to a year-round residential area. The pattern has been recorded before.

Those books also show the battles to save the river. The fight to keep the drawbridge out at Union Street so that the larger power boats are kept from the sanctuary of the upper reaches. The conflict over the pollution, especially the site of the sewage treatment plant at Scituate and the industrial pollution of the headwaters. And the long losing battle to save the river islands from development. There is also a history of the various fights to prevent the riverside gravel operations and to stop the filling of local wetlands and development along the flood plain. The battles seem endless and the war is long. Each issue flares and subsides in its turn, and while each is important, viewed in the perspective of time, a pattern begins to emerge, a series of cycles that the river has experienced.

The North River began as a tributary of an ancient river that had its mouth far beyond Massachusetts Bay in what is now the open sea. Since that time it has been subjected to the tremendous altering forces of volcanoes, glaciers, a million years of weathering and more recently though no less importantly, the works of man. The American Indian first came to the river for its abundant shellfish and the fertile soils of its watershed. He set himself shelters there, planted gardens on the high ground and for four thousand years endured in what amounted to a stable society. Then came the first of many plagues. The friendly Indians contracted smallpox or measles from the early European explorers and since they had no immunities, lost over ninety percent of their population. By the time the Pilgrims landed at Plymouth, the gardens had grown up to weeds and the villages were empty, some piled thick with the bones of the unburied.

With the settling of the white man, the cycle that had been set in motion speeded up. Within one hundred and fifty years, the river evolved from a wild estuary of Cape Cod Bay into a busy industrialized area. One hundred and fifty years after that it had returned to a semblance of its former self, and fifty years later it is threatening to decline into the open wash of sewerage that is characteristic of most of the rivers of the east coast between Boston and Washington.

So there is a cycle to the river's history, a slow rise and fall that ripples across the ages, and at present, the cycle is on a downcurve. But fortunately it has not reached bottom. Although it has many sources of pollution on its tributaries and many more impending, the North River still manages to empty clean water into Cape Cod Bay, and is still famous for its extensive beds of shellfish. And although development is crowding it at every turn, there are still quiet backwaters and sections where one can feel a remnant of sanctuary from the churning energy that pulses ceaselessly to and fro on Route 3.

But the wave is dropping, and this time around, it may not rise again. There is something very permanent about the asphalt deserts of the suburban shopping centers. Residential areas do not fluctuate as readily as industries that are dependent on local resources, and there is an element in the exurban community that endures— not only endures, but keeps evolving in its external form until it reaches a steady state m which it is no longer distinguishable from the center city. Changes like that wreak no good for rivers.

And William G. Vinal is in his house in Norwell, compiling the records of change. He has an interest in the welfare of the North River because it is the resource that nourished him. He is a product of the short hills where he raised his corn and the long marshes which gave him the hay that gave him meat. It was the circling pairs of ducks and the high calls of the shorebirds that fed his spirit. And it is the winding river that he sees behind his eyelids when he reaches back in time. For that, he hates to see it die.

From: *Running Waters*: Mass Audubon yearbook, 1977

The Legend of the Golden Fox

Setting: Boston Harbor, 1970.

The year they saw the golden fox, Mugsy got the contract to clear sticks and driftwood from Boston Harbor. He had a tough, elegant boat named *Priscilla* and not much to do with her that season, and when he got the contract, in order to celebrate, he decided to hold an Easter egg hunt on the Harbor Islands.

All this was long ago in the time before there was a Boston Harbor Islands National Recreation Area, in the years when the waterfront was unpolished and nasty, and there were plenty of stories and no lack of storytellers. Mugsy was the outsider. He was a gentleman among wharf rats, a dandy and a dreamer, who never let his aristocratic background, his money, his good looks, and his ritzy friends come between him and the drifters, the boat bums, and the sometime crooks he counted among his best friends. He was a poet manqué, a literate sort who would often shout long quotes from his one great hero, the Sea Rat in *The Wind in the Willows* while plowing around the harbor in his tug.

"I shipped myself onboard a small trading vessel bound from Constantinople," he would announce to a disparate assemblage of friends and crewmen, "by classic seas whose every wave throbs with a deathless memory, to the Grecian Islands and the Levant. Those were golden days and balmy nights!"

The wharf rats would listen suspiciously. They misunderstood poor Mugsy, but they tolerated him. He was just one more of the various eccentric types who hung around the docks, and a cut above the others at that. It was, after all, Mugsy's friend, Arthur—also a towboat captain—who claimed he liked to hire only murderers because they were loyal. "Thieves you can't trust," he used to say.

Mugsy was more discriminating. The wharf rats may have misunderstood him, but they loved his adventures, and on the day of the Easter egg hunt they all piled aboard the Priscilla and, under a bright spring sky, steamed toward the islands and Mugsy's previously secreted eggs. There was a street kid on board packing a twenty-two caliber pistol; there were a few sailors, temporarily on the beach; a down-and-out marine painter; and a few of the people who hung around Estabrook's boatyard. And there was also Serena, Mugsy's companion for that period of his life, an elegant English lady with a refined Oxford accent.

They landed at Peddocks and hunted for eggs, moved on to Georges and Lovells and hunted some more, and then, the eggs depleted, they sailed outbound toward the Brewsters. "Thence we turned and coasted up the Adriatic, its shores swimming in an atmosphere of amber, rose, and aquamarine," said Mugsy, still quoting. Someone broke open one of Mugsy's precious bottles of 1959 Château Mouton. And someone else emptied it before they reached the outer islands.

Just off Greater Brewster, Mugsy hove to and let the *Priscilla* idle in the swell.

Serena went ashore to look around, and when she came back she was in shock.

"I've seen a fox," she said. "A magnificent golden fox."

The younger ones streamed ashore, Serena in the lead, while Mugsy kept his vessel off the rocks. They climbed over bedrock and tunneled through brush to the fox's den. The kid with the gun was there, the marine painter, and the Estabrook crowd. None believed in Serena's fox, and yet as soon as they arrived at the den it poked its head up from between the rocks, scrambled to the top of a rock pile, and halted on the rise, its golden fur flowing in the sea wind.

"A real fox," shouted the kid with the gun. "Helloo foxy," called Serena. "I knew you were here." The fox looked down at the assembled band and fled over the hill, more in horror than in fear.

The kid lost control and, firing madly into the air, dashed over the hill. Back on the *Priscilla*, Mugsy, who heard the shots whistle signaled desperately for his crew to return. There was chaos and shouting. They chased the kid, caught him, and confiscated his gun, and then, still in awe of the beautiful vision beyond the squalor of the docks, returned to the *Priscilla*. It was the last anyone saw of the golden fox.

Back on board they told and retold the adventure, broke out more wine, and then steamed back to port.

Mugsy was somewhat subdued. "For now I had done with islands for the time," he quoted softly.

Things went downhill after that. At the end of the summer the man with the murderous crew got the cleanup contract. Mugsy borrowed money he couldn't repay, and that winter he disappeared to South America, never to return. The wharf rats missed him. They often talked about his Easter adventure, and even those who missed the event had visions of the golden fox, of something beautiful and good in the harbor beyond the city.

From: *Sanctuary*

PART FOUR: STRAY LEAVES FROM A WILD GARDEN

Transcripts from The Trial of Humanity

The Council of all Beings v. Home Sapiens

*Depositions from the
Witnesses for the Prosecution*

Setting: A courtroom.

MAY IT PLEASE THE COURT.

YOUR HONOR, MEMBERS OF THE JURY, I represent the Council of All Beings. It is my intention today to lay out for you the particulars of this unique and remarkable case.

But, in order to do so, I would request that you willingly suspend your powers of disbelief and imagine for one moment that the entire history of the earth is but a single day.

Put the case that in the obscure first hours before dawn of that singular day, life, in the form of self-replicating chemicals, finally appears in the warm seas that cover the earth. For the next few hours, these primitive life forms, these mere chains of genetic material, evolve into the myriad and fantastical forms that prepare the way for our own existence. At sunrise the hordes of trilobites, then the starfish, snails, amphibians, and sharks. Toward midday, the insects and reptiles, and then, in the afternoon, the great lumbering beasts of the Jurassic, followed by birds and turtles, marsupials, and then toward dusk, dolphins, whales, and the great mammals of the Cenozoic.

This world, your Honor, is a green paradise, a world characterized by a lush and verdant plant cover and populated with a diverse and abundant animal life, so rich and so complex in its interrelationships one would suppose that it could never be undone. It is a bright, living planet in an otherwise dark and dead universe.

But, your Honor, members of the jury, those of you in the gallery, put the case that in the last thirty seconds of the last minute of the last hour of that bright day, there appears on the African savanna a small bipedal primate. Over the next few seconds, this creature overruns the earth in such vast numbers that its biomass becomes greater than that of any other living entity on earth save for the swarms of krill that populate the waters of the southern oceans. And now, in the last few seconds before an uncertain midnight, that upright mammal, swelled now not only in numbers, but also by an arrogance unmatched in the history of the world, is in the process of transforming that once-living planet into a dull and lifeless rock where only a few of the most enduring species will survive.

It is my intention today to demonstrate to you the irrefutable guilt, the accountability, the blame, the unequivocal culpability of that avaricious bipedal primate for the destruction of as yet uncounted numbers of fellow species of the planet earth. I will prove that through greed, through indifference, ignorance, and in some cases through downright cruelty, the defendant did cause the extinction of some of the finest jewels of creation, beings who were the end result of millennia of slow evolution, 600 million years of procreation, of endurance, of struggle, of, we are emboldened to say, even hope and belief in a future.

Now, because of the behavior of this single species, that future is in question.

I must warn you that later in this trial, when you hear the argument for the defense, you will no doubt learn that there have been periods of vast extinctions before in the history of the world, the most notable of which was the great dying of the cretaceous period when those ill-named "terrible lizards," the dinosaurs, disappeared from the planet. You will hear that, all told, there have been five such great dyings over the 600-million-year span of life on earth. But I must tell you that never in history have extinctions occurred so fast and at such an all-encompassing rate. And never before, never in this 600-million-year period, has a single species been responsible for the extinction of another.

In order to make my case today, I will concentrate on one example, the recent history of species on the North American continent. Although close to home, North America is by no means the best example. In the Mediterranean Basin and in Africa, between 1600 and 1900, which in the scale of geologic time is a barely measurable period, vast sections of forest disappeared, resulting in the extinction of untold numbers of known, as well as unknown species—or so it is believed. No one knows for certain because no one was counting. In our time, in the tropical rain forests of the world in particular, things are moving even faster. We are losing approximately one acre of forest every second, resulting in the extinction of as yet untold numbers of species. No one knows, your Honor. No one knows, because this world, this vast and splendid tapestry of life, is only partly explored; as many as 90 percent of living species are as yet unrecorded. And yet, as you hear this brief testimony, that is to say in the period of time no more than one hour, any number of species of plants, of insects, of reptiles, amphibians, birds, and mammals may be extinguished forever from planet Earth.

I would remind you that at the root of this mass extinction is a deep and unremitting vanity, an arrogance so ingrained in the defendant, so much a part of its makeup, that it is perhaps incapable of understanding—in spite of its purported ability to reason—that it is a biological entity, and as such, is subject to biological law. What I mean to say, your Honor, is that the ultimate endangered species is the defendant itself.

Time and the laws of life are ruthless taskmasters. They cut out what does not fit, and in time—in a very short time in the scheme of things, unless we today choose to convict—they will eliminate this transgressor through natural processes. The defendant, as you will see from the evidence I intend to introduce, is imperious, haughty, and domineering, but it is not invincible. Its technology does not, cannot, and will not, deliver it from natural laws.

Already, if you would examine the evidence of history, you can see the beginnings of its demise. Other plants and animals are the source of life for this curious bipedal species. They feed it, they provide the clothing it uses to cover its body, they are the substance of the medicines it uses to cure its diseases. They add texture and diversity to the fabric of its otherwise dull life. They are the source of its recreation, they stabilize the ecosystems upon which it depends; they preserve within their genes the variety of genetic material of the small range of plants and animals the species uses to survive. And yet, in spite of this total dependence, in spite of the fact that the species could not survive a single day without its associated plants and animals, the defendant continues in its ruthless course of mass destruction.

In a certain manner, we need not judge here today. The species has already convicted itself. Biology will have its revenge.

Your Honor, members of the jury, I will be presenting now the case of North America, but I would preface my case with a brief description of the defendant. It is my belief that the evidence will show that this species is especially culpable because alone among the many creatures of earth it is believed to be capable of reason and therefore it *knows what it is doing.* Indeed, the evidence I intend now to present has been assembled *by the defendant itself.*

The following is taken from Laurence Palmer's *Field Book of Natural History,* which is a general description of common species and includes on page 702 a description of the defendant.

Exhibit A: The Defendant
PHYLUM CHORDATA. CLASS MAMMALIA
Order Primates / Family Hominidae
HOMO SAPIENS:
...Increasing rapidly in numbers in spite of the fact that a single birth per pregnancy is most common; twins occur once in every 85 births, and numbers greater than two are even more rare in occurrence. Gestation period is 250 to 285 days

with no evidence of a restricted breeding season. Male and female reach puberty between twelve and fifteen years of age. In females a 28-day reproductive cycle begins and is repeated for 30 to 35 years; a 3- to 5-day period of menstruation occurs more or less regularly unless interrupted by pregnancy. Reproductive [functions in females] cease at menopause, about age fifty. [Males] have no definite sexual cycle....

...is probably longest-lived of the mammals. Body temperature about 98.6°F. Pulse 60 to 80. Respiration 15 to 20. Hearing range 12,000 to 17,000; voice 40 to 1,152 cps. Speed, to almost 20 mph in short distance.

...Acquires 5 percent of mature weight during intrauterine life and 95 percent during a postnatal growth period of 20 to 25 years. During first year, baby increases 50 percent in length and 200 percent in weight.

...Walks upright on two limbs.. ...possesses two great compartments in the trunk, the thoracic and the abdominal cavities...distinctive feature... is the development of a brain far beyond those of predecessors in thinking and reasoning powers. Because of ability... to modify immediate environment...is not confined to the warmer and milder climates... travels on or under the sea, over the land, in the air, and now into space to the moon.

…Distinguished as an animal which is a primate that evolved from the less specialized apelike creatures from which the chimpanzee, orangutan, and gorilla also probably evolved…has a language capable of communicating very abstract ideas… not only makes but…uses tools.

By way of background, I want to introduce evidence of the historical attitudes of the defendant. This document was assembled by Clive Ponting who is currently honorary research fellow in residence at University College, Swansea, in the United Kingdom. He is the author of several works of history including, *The Right to Know: The Inside Story of the Belgrano Affair* and 1940: *Myth and Reality*. This account appears in Ponting's book *A Green History of the World*.

Exhibit B: Historical Attitudes

A reduction in wildlife habitats and extinction of species on a local scale can be identified from the time of the first human settlements. In the Nile valley the extension of the cultivated area, the draining of marshland and the organized hunting of animals led to the elimination of many species originally native to the area. By the time of the Old Kingdom (2950-2350 BC) animals such as elephants, rhinoceroses and giraffes had disappeared from the valley. The spread of settlement around the Mediterranean produced the same results with the destruction concentrated on the vulnerable animals at the top of the food chain. By about 200 BC the lion and leopard were extinct in Greece and the coastal areas of Asia Minor, and wolves and jackals were confined to the remote mountainous areas. The trapping of beavers in northern Greece had also driven them to extinction. The Roman addiction to the deliberate killing of wild animals in games and other spectacles added to the slaughter. The scale of the continuing destruction to amuse the crowds across the Roman empire, year after year, for centuries, can be guessed at from the fact that 9,000 captured animals were killed during the 100 day celebration of the dedication of the Coliseum in Rome and 11,000 were slain to mark Trajan's conquest of the new province of Dacia. By the early centuries AD, the elephant, rhinoceros and zebra were extinct in north Africa, the hippopotamus in the lower Nile and the tiger in north Persia and Mesopotamia.

The great spectacles of the Roman empire ceased in western Europe after the fifth century but the destruction of wildlife continued in other ways. Early medieval Europe consisted mainly of large areas of virtually undisturbed natural ecosystems with a small population living within it in scattered settlements (the exact opposite of the later landscape). The expansion of the settled area gradually reduced the habitats on which the plants and animals depended for their survival. Whole species became extinct and others disappeared across large areas or were severely reduced in numbers. The aurochs (the wild ancestor of modern cattle) was a woodland animal that suffered particularly from deforestation. It was extinct in Britain about 2000 c and slowly disappeared from the rest of the continent. The last known specimen died in the Jaktorowa forest in Poland in 1627. The European bison was still found in the early medieval period across a wide area of Belgium and Germany but by the eighteenth century it was only found in eastern Europe and the last wild animal died in the Bialowieza forest of Poland in 1920. The great auk, a flightless seabird, was once found in huge colonies along the Atlantic coasts of Scotland, the Western Isles, Orkney and Shetland and Iceland. It was a highly vulnerable prey—in one episode in 1540 two ships were filled with freshly killed auks in half an hour (producing five tons of salted birds) and the crew killed more birds to eat fresh. The eggs were also eaten by sailors and since the auk only laid one egg a year, its ability to breed was easily undermined. By the eighteenth century the bird was becoming rare around the British coast. The last pair were killed in Iceland in 1844.

Many more species which were once common in the whole of Europe have become extinct across large areas of the continent. Wolves were found in large numbers throughout western Europe until about 500 years ago. As late as 1420 and 1438 wolf packs were seen in the streets of Paris in daylight. In 1520 enough still survived for Francis I to organize official hunts and about a hundred years later in 1640 there are accounts of wolves coming down from the hills of the Jura to terrorise the inhabitants of Besançon. In Britain there were still enough wolves to warrant full scale hunts in Scotland during the sixteenth century. The last recorded sighting of a wolf came in 1486 in England, 1576 in Wales, in Scotland in 1743 and in Ireland during the early nineteenth century. The Brown Bear was also common across medieval western Europe (although it had died out in Britain by the tenth century). However, numbers declined steadily through hunting and destruction of its habitat and it now only survives in a few remote mountainous areas. The same pattern of events affected the beaver, which was also common in medieval Europe and was trapped for its fur. It died out in Britain as early as the thirteenth century and later across most of the rest of Europe....

While some of this trail of destruction was the side effect of agriculture and some the deliberate result of hunting and commercial exploitation, it is also evident from contemporary texts that the idea of conservation and the preservation of wildlife was mainly noticeable by its absence until comparatively recent times. The general attitude towards the natural world was well summed up by the seventeenth century English clergyman, Edmund Hickeringill, who wrote that, 'So noisome and offensive are some animals to human kind, that it concerns all mankind to get quit of the annoyance, with as speedy a riddance and despatch as may be, by any lawful means....'

In case there is any lingering doubt as to the ability of the defendant to destroy all or any species it chooses, whenever or wherever it chooses, I would submit the following documents, which are a brief history of the most populous bird ever to have lived on planet Earth.

Exhibit C: Passenger Pigeon

From *The Passenger Pigeon* by A. W. Schorger, page 11, an early account from Louisiana.

There are such prodigious numbers of pigeons that I do not fear exaggerating when I assert that they sometimes darken the sun. One day I was on the bank of the Mississippi which they were following in a flock the length of the woods. This flock was so long that having fired my first shot, I had time to reload three times; but the rapidity of their flight was so great that although I am not a bad shot, my four discharges knocked down only two.

These birds come to Louisiana only in winter, and remain in Canada during the summer, where they eat the grain like they do acorns in Louisiana.... Although what I have said of these birds up to the present is sufficient to show that their number exceeds what can be said, I wish to give an instance which proves their prodigious abundance and at the same time shows their ingenuity in securing food."

From *The Passenger Pigeon* by A. W. Schorger, page 54.

The immense flocks of passenger pigeons twisting and undulating over the landscape were spectacular—even awesome. The earth was darkened by their numbers causing chickens to start to their roost prematurely. Their dung fell like hail, leaving a characteristic odor in the air. The large flights caused fear in man and beast unaccustomed to them. Geikie, whether fictitiously or not, mentions a hunter who threw himself to the ground in terror of the thousands of birds that brushed past him. The English geologist Featherstonhaugh wrote of a flight in northeastern Arkansas in November, 1834:

> But when such myriads of timid birds as the wild pigeon are on the wing, often wheeling and performing evolutions almost as complicated as pyrotechnic movements, and creating whirlwinds as they move, they present an image of the most

fearful power. Our horse, Missouri, at such times has been so cowed by them that he would stand still and tremble in his harness, whilst we ourselves were glad when their flight was directed from us.

From *The Passenger Pigeon* by A. W. Schorger, page 145.

The *Plattsburg Republican* of August 2, 1851, estimated that not less than 150,000 dozen or 1,800,000 pigeons were sent to market from the nesting near Plattsburg, New York, in 1851. The dealers paid from 31 to 56 cents a dozen. From 15 to 25 people were employed in dressing the birds for which labor they received about eight cents per dozen.

In the spring of 1861, up to April 5, 750 barrels of 212,500 pigeons, weighing 67.5 tons, were shipped east from Circleville, Ohio, by express. In addition to the large numbers consumed locally, wagonloads were taken to Columbus, and many sent to Cincinnati.

The pigeon trade became thoroughly organized in the latter half of the nineteenth century. The large commission houses had buyers and trappers in the field and followed the movements of the pigeons the year around. Some of the large dealers were: Henry Knapp, Utica, New York; H. T. Phillips and Company, Detroit; Bond and Ellsworth, Chicago; Holmes and Sears, Chicago; Edward T. Martin, Chicago; W. P. Thomas, Peoria, Illinois; and N. W. Judy and Company, St. Louis.

Exhibit D: Demise

From *Wildlife in America* by Peter
Matthiessen, pages 158 to 160.

According to the committee report [of the
Ohio state senate]: "The passenger pigeon needs
no protection. Wonderfully prolific, having the
vast forests of the North as its breeding grounds,
traveling hundreds of miles in search of food, it
is here today and elsewhere tomorrow, and no
ordinary destruction can lessen them or be missed
from the myriads that are yearly produced." And
one cannot deny that the report seemed bulwarked
by the several immense nestings that occurred
thereafter, including one in the sandy scrub oak
barrens of south central Wisconsin in 1871, and
another one, better known, at Petoskey, Michigan,
in 1878.

The Wisconsin nesting was the largest ever described, and its awesome dimensions have been
placed at seventy-five by ten to fifteen miles,
an area of no less than seven hundred and fifty
square miles. Assuming a minimum average of
twenty-five trees per acre and five pairs per tree,
this single nesting was shared by 136,000,000
birds. This is little more than one-twentieth the
size of the flight described by Alexander Wilson,
but it is nonetheless a prodigious number, and the
predators, white, Indian, and animal, swarmed

down upon the roosts from every direction. The recent invention of the telegraph had speeded the glad news into all the adjoining states, and there were literally thousands of hunters and trappers on hand, armed variously with net, fire, and shot, as well as with an assortment of homemade contrivances designed to perform the most heroic destruction in the shortest possible time.

The area was laid waste. Hundreds of thousands, indeed millions, of dead birds were shipped out at a wholesale price of fifteen to twenty-five cents a dozen, on the cars of the same railroads which, by opening the great eastern markets, were accommodating the exit of the bison. The season, commencing in April, was profitable for only a month, and by June the markets were glutted, the pigeons were scattered, and the hunters had largely departed, leaving behind a rancid wasteland of ground white with guano, of broken trees, nests, eggs, and blue-feathered, fly-blown forms too shattered to ship, of starving squabs, of maggots and silent fur-clawed and beaked prowlers.

The Petoskey nesting was the last great congregation of passenger pigeons ever beheld on earth, and their subsequent decline was swift.

The last wild pigeon in Wisconsin was taken in 1899, and though stray individuals were seen fleetingly for another five or six years, and a captive bird survived until 1914, the last wild pigeon, for scientific purposes, is thought to be a specimen killed at Sargents, Pike County, Ohio, on the fourth day of spring, in 1900. *Wuskowhan*, the wanderer, as the Narragansett Indians had called the most numerous bird ever to exist on earth, had been whirled into the vortex of extinction.

Members of the jury, I request that you examine the following evidence prepared by Kenneth Mallory and Les Kaufman of the New England Aquarium in Boston, Massachusetts, for a public lecture series sponsored by the Lowell Institute and published under the title The Last Extinction. The material speaks for itself, but bear in mind that the list includes species and subspecies but does not include invertebrates such as mollusks, insects, spiders, crustaceans, sponges, corals, and jellyfish. Nor does it include plants.

Exhibit F: Extinct Vertebrates

Extinct Vertebrates of the United States,
U.S. Territories, and Canada since 1492

FISHES: Miller Lake lamprey, 1953; Longjaw cisco, 1970s; Deepwater cisco, 1950s; Blackfin cisco, 1960s; Yellowfin cutthroat trout, 1910; Silver trout, 1930s; Thicktail chub, 1957; Pahrangat spinedace, 1940; Phantom shiner, 1975; Bluntnose shiner, 1964; Clear Lake splittail, 1970; Las Vegas dace, 1950s; June sucker, 1935; Snake River sucker, 1928; Harelip sucker, 1900; Tecopa pupfish, 1942;

Shoshone pupfish, 1966, Raycraft Ranch killifish, 1960; Pahrump Ranch killifish, 1960; Pahrump Ranch killifish, 1956; Ash Meadows killifish, 1957; Whiteline topminnow, 1900; Amistad gambusia, 1977; Blue pike, 1971; Utah Lake sculpin, 1928; Lake Ontario kiyi, 1967; Alvord cutthroat, 1940; Maravillas red shiner, 1960; Independence Valley tui chub, 1970; Banff longnose dace, 1982; Grass Valley speckled dace, 1950; San Marcos gambusia, 1983.

AMPHIBIANS: Relict leopard frog, 1960; Golden coqui, 1980s; Web-footed cocqui, 1980s.

REPTILES: Navassa iguana, 1800s; Iguana, 1800s; St. Croix racer, 1900s.

BIRDS: Labrador duck, 1878; Heath hen, 1932; Kusaie crake, 1828; Laysan rail, 1944; Hawaiian brown rail, 1964; Hawaiian spotted rail, 1893; Wake island rail, 1945; great auk, 1844; Passenger pigeon, 1914; Culebra Puerto Rican parrot, 1899; Mauge's parakeet, 1892; Carolina parakeet, 1914; Louisiana parakeet, 1912; Virgin Islands screech owl, 1980; San Clementa Bewick's wren, 1927; Lanai thrush, 1931; Oahu thrush, 1825; Laysan millerbird, 1923; Kioea, 1859; Oahu oo, 1837; Molokai oo, 1915; Hawaii oo, 1934; Santa Barbara song sparrow, 1967; Texas Henslow's sparrow, 1983; Laysan apapane, 1923; Hawaiian mamo, 1898; Black mamo, 1907; Lanai akialoa, 1894; Oahu akialoa, 1837; Hawaii akialoa, 1895; Oahu nukupu'u, 1860; Oahu akepa, 1893; Greater amakihi, 1900; Lanai creeper, 1937;

Ula-ai-hawane, 1892; Greater Kona finch, 1896; Lesser Kona finch, 1891; Kona finch, 1894; Kusaie starling, 1828; Dusky seaside sparrow, 1987; Amak song sparrow, 1980.

MAMMALS: Puerto Rican shrew, 1500; Puerto Rican long-nosed bat, 1900?; Puerto Rican long-tongued bat, 1900?; Puerto Rican ground sloth, 1500; Penasco chipmunk, 1980; Tacoma pocket gopher, 1970; Goff's pocket gopher, 1955; Sherman's pocket gopher, 1950; Pallid beach mouse, 1946; Giant deer mouse, 1870; Chadwick Beach cottonmouse, 1950; Gull Island vole, 1898; Louisiana vole, 1905; Puerto Rican hutia, 1500; Puerto Rican paca, 1500; Lessert Puerto Rican agouti, 1500; Greater Puerto Rican agouti, 1500; Atlantic gray whale, 1750; Southern California kit fox, 1903; Florida red wolf, 1925; Texas red wolf; 1970; Kenai Peninsula wolf, 1910; Newfoundland wolf, 1911; Banks Island wolf, 1920; Cascade Mountains wolf; 1940; Northern Roicky Mountain wolf; 1940; Mongollon Mountains wolf, 1942; Texas gray wolf, 1942; Great Plains wolf, 1926; Southern Rocky Mountain wolf, 1935; California grizzly bear, 1925; Sea Minkj, 1890; Wisconsin cougar, 1925; Caribbean monk seal, 1960; Steller's sea cow, 1768; Eastern elk, 1880; Merriam's elk, 1906; Queen Charlotte caribou, 1935, Badlands bighorn, 1910.

Your Honor, members of the jury, I call to the stand Mark Jerome Walters. Dr. Walters is a veterinarian and a specialist on the conservation of endangered species. His most recent book, A Shadow and a Song (Chelsea Green, 1992), chronicles the extinction of the dusky seaside sparrow from the day the bird was first described in the late 1800s to the moment of the last individual's death in 1987. Walters founded and directs The Requiem Project, which is devoted to preserving the accounts of vanishing plants and animals. He most recently served as a biodiversity conservation analyst with the US Agency for International Development in Washington, DC.

Exhibit G: The Meaning of Extinction

I recently visited the Smithsonian museum in Washington, DC, where corridors are lined with dioramas and display cases of extinct species. In one display, nine stuffed passenger pigeons perch on a branch against a painted autumn backdrop of a beech-oak forest in the Appalachian mountains. This pigeon, as you have heard, once may have been the most abundant bird in the world. A nearby case displays Martha, the last passenger pigeon, who died in captivity at the Cincinnati Zoological Gardens on September 1, 1914.

Below Martha is a reconstructed skeleton of a stocky flightless bird known as the dodo from the island of Mauritius in the Indian Ocean. In

1681, within a century of its discovery, hunters wiped out the dodo. Also on display is the great auk, a species that once lived in the far north and wintered as far south as Florida; the last was killed in 1844. A few specimens over is a case displaying a pair of heath hens. A staple food of the early New England colonists, the birds were so common in the wooded areas of early Boston that they were often served for dinner several times a week. By 1927, disease, bad weather, poachers, and legions of feral cats had reduced the number to about a dozen. In 1932, the last heath hen was seen.

Many other species are in those cases at the Smithsonian. But, in fact, only a part of the museum's collection of extinct species is in public view.

Tucked away in drawers, among many others, are skins of the last dusky seaside sparrows, birds that once lived in the salt marshes along the Indian and Banana rivers of east central Florida. In the 1960s, the Kennedy Space Center was built in dusky habitat.

For a time, your Honor, the birds lived in the shadow of Launch Complex 39, the spot from which humans were first launched to the moon. But, because the salt marsh bred bothersome mosquitoes that hampered the space program, the land was diked and permanently flooded to destroy the insects' breeding areas. The sparrow's breeding areas were flooded as well. Housing developments, highways, and wildfires finally did in the rest. The last dusky seaside sparrow died in captivity, near Orlando, in 1987. I trust the Court will not overlook the inherent irony of this particular case.

The Greek scholar Dionysius of Halicarnassus said that history is philosophy learned from examples. What does the passenger pigeon say to us? What does the great auk whisper? Can the dodo tell us anything we do not already know? The dusky? We will never know until we consider past extinctions with far greater deliberation than we have so far.

We now have an economic philosophy. We have a philosophy of government. But we have yet to develop a philosophy toward extinction. We barely have learned to grieve. Indeed, as Aldo Leopold wrote, "For one species to mourn the death of another is a new thing under the sun." How do we begin to shape examples of extinction and our growing awareness of loss into a philosophy of caring for all life? How do we chart a positive course from a history of annihilation?

Rarely are the lessons of history explicit. But perhaps Martha tells us that numbers alone are no assurance against extinction. Abundance should not decrease an animal's value in our eyes. Ten million bison on a western plain are no less deserving of our protective care than the last twenty in a zoo.

Science can teach us cause and effect, but only philosophy can teach the meaning of kinship; that interconnectedness means more than mere mutual dependency. Dionysius might have told us that the extinction of the dusky seaside sparrow teaches us that outward journeys even to the moon— can never take us as far as inward ones; that searching is different from seeking; and that facts about the universe are no substitute for a philosophy of caring for life on earth.

The litany of extinctions can teach us how to feel about the loss of species. We mourn the death of individuals, but no rituals mark the passing of a species. Death is the end of a life, but extinction is the end of birth. Holmes Rolston, III, wrote, "Extinction kills essences beyond existences—the soul as well as the body. To superkill a species is to shut down a story of millennia and leave no future possibilities."

After spending the morning around the glass display cases at the Smithsonian, I rode the metro across town to the National Zoo. I saw the giant panda, palm cockatoos, tigers, cheetahs, mountain gorillas, and the endangered Guam rail. I stood before these endangered species as people must have once stood before the last living passenger pigeons.

I suddenly imagined the Smithsonian entry hall two centuries from now, a stuffed black-and-white bearish creature poses in a gallery of plastic bamboo. A sign reads: Giant panda. Thousands once roamed the clouded highland forests in parts of China. Habitat transformed by farming. The last specimen died in captivity in Wolong, China, in 2115. In the museum's corridors, the display cases have multiplied. They hold a Bachman's warbler, a Guam rail, a palm cockatoo, a hyacinth macaw, and hundreds of newcomers. In the Gallery of Extinct Mammals is a Bengal tiger, a cheetah, and numerous other animals.

But celebrities such as the giant panda do not necessarily teach the realities of extinction. It is the little things that run the world. For every endangered large mammal, tens of thousands of plants, invertebrates, and little-known birds languish in anonymity.

Not far from the panda yard—in a small feeder spring along Rock Creek, which defines a portion of the zoo's boundary, there is an endangered species known as the Hay's spring amphipod. Almost no one knows about this shrimplike crustacean. Hundreds could fit in the palm of your hand, and it is little noted in the drama of endangered species conservation. If it became extinct tomorrow, who would know or care? Is there anything to learn from an animal we barely knew was here? If we are unaware of the examples that matter most, how are we to find a philosophy that matters at all?

If Dionysius is right, even as many species become extinct, a philosophy of caring learned from the examples of loss is still something we have every reason to hope for. What is philosophy but lessons learned the hard way?

May it please the Court. I want to introduce a passage from Professor E. O. Wilson's latest book, *The Diversity of Life*. As I hope you have surmised from the testimony, the tapestry of life is made of many threads, the weave (not to mention the Ultimate Weaver) is ill-understood, the strands delicate and easily parted, and the whole cloth in jeopardy. There is perhaps no greater authority on this complex question of the diversity of life than Professor Edward O. Wilson. He is the Curator of Entomology at Harvard University's Museum of Comparative Zoology and is the author of several books on the subject of biological diversity. He is also, among other things, one of the world authorities on ants.

Exhibit H: A New Ethic
From *The Diversity of Life* by Edward O. Wilson, page 351.

Signals abound that the loss of life's diversity endangers not just the body but the spirit. If that much is true, the changes occurring now will visit harm on all generations to come.

The ethical imperative should therefore be, first of all, prudence. We should judge every scrap of biodiversity as priceless while we learn to use it and come to understand what it means to humanity. We should not knowingly allow any species or race to go extinct. And let us go beyond mere salvage to begin the restoration of natural environments, in order to enlarge wild populations and stanch the hemorrhaging of biological wealth. There can be no purpose more enspiriting than to begin the age of restoration, reweaving the wondrous diversity of life that still surrounds us.

The evidence of swift environmental change calls for an ethic uncoupled from other systems of belief. Those committed by religion to believe that life was put on earth in one divine stroke will recognize that we are destroying the Creation, and those who perceive biodiversity to be the product of blind evolution will agree. Across the other great philosophical divide, it does not matter whether species have independent rights or, conversely, that moral reasoning is uniquely a human concern. Defenders of both premises seem destined to gravitate toward the same position on conservation.

The stewardship of environment is a domain on the near side of metaphysics where all reflective persons can surely find common ground. For what, in the final analysis, is morality but the command of conscience seasoned by a rational examination of consequences? And what is a fundamental precept but one that serves all generations? An enduring environmental ethic will aim to preserve not only the health and freedom of our species, but access to the world in which the human spirit was born.

Summation

In closing I will remind you, as the common parlance has it, that extinction is forever. It is the death of birth. We may lose our mountains to volcanoes, our shorelines to the seas, our forests to wildfire, but once a species has disappeared from the world, another heaven and another earth must pass before such a one can be again. There is only one reason why the species of our time are disappearing from Earth at such an alarming rate, and that is because they are being exterminated by the defendant. There can be no refuting of this truth, no turning from this reality. None of the great spiritual monuments of its history, neither its cathedrals, nor its symphonic hymns, nor its great works of literature and art can abrogate the singular fact that this species did knowingly and willingly homogenize a once biologically diverse planet.

Members of the jury, the primate is guilty. It is guilty because it had a choice, if for no other reason. It is capable of logic; it is a rational being, a thinking animal, and, in spite of this, it diminished the world.

Your Honor, members of the jury, I rest my case.

From: Notes from reprints from various
publications and *Sanctuary*.

The Fox Hunters' Debate

Setting: Long Island, New York, 1830.

Anyone who has ever studied law will know of the sad story of Mr. Lodovick Post, who one fine morning in the year of our Lord 1805, set out with his hounds and horse in pursuit of what the law books refer to as a beast *fera natura*, which is to say, a wild animal. The beast in this case was a red fox, an animal despised by Mr. Post, the plaintiff in this particular case, and also by the defendant, a certain Mr. Pierson.

On the day in question, Mr. Lodovick Post, a country gentleman of some means, had mounted his steed at the crack of dawn and with hounds and horn, rode out in pursuit of the "wily quadruped," as the dissent termed it. Toward evening, having pursued the windings of Sir Fox the day long, and weary with hunting, Squire Post closed in on his prey, whereupon Mr. Pierson, who had not shared in the labors, nor the honors, of the hunt, appeared on the scene.

This Pierson, this "saucy intruder," drew his fusil, took aim, shot the fox, and made off with it.

Who owns the fox? Mr. Post, who chased it all day, who tore through brambles, who sweated, who went without lunch, who was stiff with riding, whose hounds were hoarse, breathless, and scratched? Or Mr. Pierson, who happened upon a tired fox and shot it?

Post took Pierson to court, claiming ownership, and won his case. Pierson appealed, and there rose a mighty furor over the poor, long-dead fox, who by this time was reduced to a mere pelt. Counsels for both parties reached deep into history to make their points, citing, among others, the Roman emperor Justinian, whose laws held that pursuit alone vests no property. Pierson's counsel argued that the fact that Post rode after the fox all day meant nothing, mere pursuit gave no legal right to ownership, he argued, and the fox in fact became the possession of Pierson as soon as he killed it. Post's counsel countered that whatever Justinian thought about foxes was insignificant. He argued that these were modern times (1805!), and society had changed since the days of Rome; and, if society changes, should not also laws change?

Post lost the case, Pierson got his fox after all, and *Pierson v. Post* went on to become a seminal case in the annals of American property law.

But the dissent bears watching. In our time (1995), in a world in which "resources" (a loaded, anthropocentric word if ever there was one) are shrinking, who in fact does own the fox? Sir Fox, were he with us now, would surely argue that he is his own man ʒand beholden to nobody but his wife and little ones, and the native people of this continent might have agreed.

Nicolas Perrot, who spent time among the Indian hunters of the Great Lakes region in the eighteenth century, wrote that a man returning from a hunt, no matter how long or laborious it may have been, was bound by tradition to *share* his catch with the other members of his tribe. The custom was so ingrained that hungry huntsmen would sometimes hide their kill in the forest and butcher it alone so as not to have to divide the booty.

And if the ownership of a fox or any other quarry is in question, it's not much of a jump to wonder who owns the land.

Chief Tecumseh, of the Shawnee, whose people successfully lived on the American continent for some fifteen thousand years or more without actually owning a scrap of it, came to the heart of the issue in 1812. "Sell a country!" he said. "Why not sell the air, the clouds, and the great sea as well as the earth?"

From: *Trespassing*, 1996

Bear Lore

Setting: Bear rituals in the Northern Hemisphere.

Up until the 1960s hunters of the indigenous Ainu culture of Hokkaido, Japan, would trap a bear cub, bring it to the village and raise it, feeding it human food or, if it was still young enough, feed it with a wet nurse. After two or three years, in a ceremony accompanied by ritual chanting and dances, they would tie it to a post and shoot it with arrows. Then they would decorate the bear and a local young woman would marry the bear.

Bear lore of this sort was also common throughout the Northern Hemisphere. In the folklore of certain North American native tribes, there are stories of marriages between a bear and a woman and folktales of tamed bears and bear marriages occur throughout the Northern Hemisphere

In Western European cultures it appears in the folk stories of Goldilocks and the Three Bears, as well as Rose Red and Snow White, in which a bear is taken in by a human family one winter. The two daughters make friends with him. Of course in the end, the "bear" turns out to be a prince, under the spell of an evil dwarf.

There is even a body of bear lore in ancient Greece. Artemis, the hunter goddess, had a school for girls who were associated with bears. And there is an ancient cycle of folk tales of a figure known as the "Bearson." In this story, which also occurs among Native American tribes of the American West, a bear marries a local woman and the two take up residence in the bear's cave. In time, she gives birth to a son. But the bear husband learns from a soothsayer that the son will grow up and kill him. So the bear rolls a huge rock in front of the cave mouth and imprisons his wife and child. He goes out to hunt every day and brings food back to his little family. Eventually, the bear's son grows into a very strong young man and one day he manages to roll the huge rock aside and escapes, freeing his mother. Some years later he encounters his father, and true to the prediction, kills him in a fight.

Over the years the Bearson was incorporated into other folktales. He became an infamous trickster, the hero of many pre-Hellenic Greek folktales. Scholars have argued that the Odyssey is in part a collection of folk tales in which the hero, Odysseus, replays the roles of the traditional trickster of lore, along the lines of the Bearson. The most direct link to this would be the story of the giant Cyclops, Polyphemus, who traps Odysseus and his men in his cave along with his flock of sheep. The crew fashion a sharp stick and use it to blind the giant, and then escapes by clinging to the under-belly of the sheep when Polyphemus rolls the rock door aside to let his sheep out to graze.

There is another folkloric twist to this tale. When asked his name, Odysseus tells Polyphemus he is called "Otus." The word in ancient Greek means "nobody" but it also is close to the word for "owl." Athena's totem animal was the owl, the bird of wisdom. Hearing the cries of Polyphemus, his fellow giants arrive and ask who is hunting him. "Nobody," Polyphemus says. So they go away.

In the Native American version of this cycle of myths the bear is not so bad. He does marry a human female, but their children grow up to be strong leaders.

In the pre-contact period in North America there was a local folk tale about a shaman named Paukawna, who could turn himself into a bear. He lived on for centuries, either as a man, or a bear.

The legend even carried on up into the 19th century and was recorded in various histories of the Scratch Flat region. In this version, around 1812, a free African-American man named Johnnie Putnam was living in a cabin in a woodlot on a ridge on the eastern edge of the tract. One winter night his dog began whimpering and scratching at the door to be let in, and the next morning Putnam noticed the tracks of a large animal circling the little house. He followed the tracks and saw the huge form of a black bear resting halfway up a hemlock tree in the woodlot.

Putnam ran to the house of Joel Proctor, the owner of the woodlot, and the two of them returned to the woods. The bear was still there, apparently sound asleep, whereupon Proctor raised his gun, took aim, and shot the bear, who tumbled dead at Johnnie Putnam's feet. Proctor told Johnnie to wait while he got his ox team hooked up to drag the bear's body home, and Johnnie sat down, leaned against the tree, and took out his pipe for a smoke. While he waited, the bear began to stir, and then, suddenly, leaped to its feet and began stumbling around the hemlock grove, sometimes raising itself on two feet, and yowling and screaming in a most hideous manner, until finally, spent, it dropped again to the ground and died.

This incident somehow undid Johnnie Putnam. In some versions of the tale, he joined up with Proctor and went off to fight in the War of 1812. He came back a changed man and settled back in his cabin to live out his days in solitude. He never spoke again about the bear incident until shortly before his death, when he for whatever reason, retold his tale with a detail he had never shared, not even with Proctor.

"Wasn't no bear died that day," he is recorded as saying, "was a man."

From: *Ceremonial Time,* 1984

Bird of the Dreadful Night

Setting: the Protestant cemetery, Porto San Paolo, Rome.

One rainy night in Rome in 1910, the famous Swedish physician and author Axel Munthe was involved in a somewhat nefarious transfer of bodies from a grave in the Protestant cemetery at Porta San Paolo. He and the grave digger were hard at work when, out of the gloom, from behind the Cestius Pyramid, a big owl began to call. Munthe was a great lover of owls and birds in general. He traveled in the highest social circles, was classically educated and a skilled physician, but a chill shot through him nonetheless. He knew owls were the traditional harbingers of death.

Just before the Roman emperor Antoninus died, an owl had alighted on his residence. Same thing happened to Valentinian, according to Roman histories. And, before the death of the great Augustus, an owl called out.

Later in history, the Italians had their revenge by consuming owls or using them in net lures, but even in Munthe's time, and well into the twentieth century, Italian peasants traveling at night would cross themselves or touch a crucifix if they heard an owl call.

Owls fare no better in English and northern European folklore. You couldn't even mention owls in Munthe's native Sweden without putting yourself at risk of a sorcerer's charm, and killing one was sure to bring on ill luck. Throughout northern Europe and even into the Near East, owls were considered the associates of witches, or dark deeds, harbingers of a death to come, and were even used as ingredients in witches' brews.

Shakespeare's weird sisters used an owlet's wing to strengthen their foul concoction in *Macbeth*, and later in the play, an owl—"the fatal bellman"— shrieks as Macbeth commits yet another murder in scene two of the second act. No doubt the scream of that notorious Irish herald of death, the banshee, had its origin in the wail of the Irish barn owl.

Curiously, there are only two exceptions to the owls' bad reputation.

In ancient Greece the owl was considered a sacred bird, associated with wisdom and the goddess Athena.

In fact, in some of the statues of Athena, the goddess appears with an owl's head. This association with intelligence was used in the wordplay in the Polyphemus tale.

The other cultures that appear to have a certain reverence for owls are certain tribes of American Indians.

Archaeologists, excavating a 5,000-year-old rock shelter not far from Marlboro, Massachusetts, found, among the bones of more edible species, the tiny hollow bones of a screech owl. The owl could have been used for ceremonial purposes, or perhaps was even kept as a pet. In historic times, there are records of pet owls kept by the Mandans in the Missouri River valley; and the Zuni, who had a special appreciation for owls, used to keep them in their houses. On a darker side, shamans in certain Midwestern tribes used to transform themselves into owls in order to attack their enemies.

None of these mystic emanations should be surprising to anyone who has ever been awakened by the shivering descent of a screech-owl call at midnight just beyond the bedroom window, let alone the bizarre, strangled caterwauling of a barred owl from a nearby wooded swamp.

From: *Sanctuary*

A Dog of Singular Intent

Setting: Scratch Flat

There are three species of rat in New England: the black rat, the Norway rat, and the wood rat. The latter is a now-rare native that generally prefers forested areas away from houses. It is distinguished from the other two by its furred tail and the fact that, in contrast to its fellow rats, it is fair-minded. It likes to decorate its nest with shining objects such as coins or wedding rings but will graciously leave a gift to replace the stolen item—a pebble, for example.

The black rat is more of a rogue. It favors seaport towns and docks, and is the rat that was responsible for the spread of the Black Death in the 14th century.

The Norway rat is the common city rat of sewers and streets, although it can also be found in the country, around barns and farmyards. A few years ago, a Norway rat took up residence under the floor of a glassed-in conservatory at our house that serves as a dining room. The other resident animal in our house at that time was a dog, a Jack Russell terrier, a breed known for its boundless energy, its singular perseverance in the face of a mission, and the fact that it despises rats. Perhaps needless to say, the presence of these two species in more or less the same quarters did not bode well for the rat.

Said rat arrived at our house in the dead of a cold winter and selected a crawl space beneath the dining room for its living quarters. We could see him from time to time, feeding like a chipmunk beneath the nearby bird feeder, and, from the perspective of the breakfast table, he didn't look particularly evil or vicious. He had a healthy brown coat and appeared to be nothing more than a benign wild animal, but the persistence of the dog inevitably led to an ill-fated course of events.

Inasmuch as this particular dog was a Jack Russell, once he smelled the rat, he became obsessed. He lost interest in the primary pleasure of his small life—food—and took up the cause, moving into the dining room. He posted himself above the rat's resting places, whining and scratching the floor. He would leave from time to time, eat quickly, and then return to his work. We always knew exactly where the rat was under the floor since the dog would move to different spots around the room, snuffling and scratching.

He actually began to lose weight—such was his obsession. So we had to act, in order to preserve the health of our guardian companion animal.

I set out a live trap, but the rat was too smart to enter. I blocked all the holes that would allow access to the foundation and jammed the trap in the exit and entrance he appeared to be using. Somehow he got around the obstacle.

I staked the dog near the feeder, which suited him perfectly. He stood guard all day long, staring intently and whining at the rat hole—which, of course, alerted the rat that this was not the best of times to come out and feed.

Finally, I gave up and bought a regular rat trap.

I caught the rat the next morning and immediately regretted what I had done. He had been, enfin, a healthy wild animal, just trying to get by. Nevertheless, I reasoned that we alien Cro-Magnons got here in North America ten thousand years before he did and were therefore more native than he—Norway rats did not arrive in the New World until the late 17th century.

That was not the end of the dog and rat saga, however. I calculated that our guard needed what human psychologists refer to as "closure." So with the Jack Russell leaping at my waist to get at his prey, I carried the lifeless rat to a clear spot in the yard and flung him out across the icy snow. He skidded along as if fleeing, pursued by the dog, who caught him, gave him a death-dealing shake, and tossed him aside, his mission accomplished.

I never told him it was not he who had killed the rat.

From: *An Eden of Sorts,* 2019

The Wolf

Setting: Bushwhacking from Westford to Concord: Halfway to Concord with my fellow travelers, Kata and Barkley, we hit an impassable marsh and come upon a young boy and his sister, selling apples.

Just beyond the stream we come to another small rural road called South Street. On the other side of the road the brook opens into a marsh, and so we walk north to get to some high ground we can see from the road. Just opposite the wooded area we see children sitting at a table in front of a house, selling apples. There are two of them, a boy of about twelve with neatly combed short hair and his sister, a younger child of about eight. They have set up little boxes of apples, some jugs of cider, and also individual apples on a card table covered with a white sheet.

A sign beside the table announces APPLE FOR SALE.

Kata insists on buying a few.

"How's business?" she asks.

"A little slow, actually," the boy answers.

"Did you grow these?" Kata asks.

"My father grew some," the girl says, "and we bought the cider at the mill."

"He didn't exactly grow them," the boy interrupts.

"The tree grew them. He just picked them."

"I picked them too," the girl says.

"We'll take four," Barkley says and begins fishing for money.

A gray minivan drives by slowly and the boy calls out, "Apples for sale." The van slows but moves on.

"That's what they all do," he says. "They just look."

"Well, in the old days you would have had a lot of people like us, just walking by," Kata says. "They would have bought. Cars don't buy things."

"Cars can't buy, actually," the boy says.

"Are you, by any chance, intending to enter the law, by way of a career?" Barkley asks.

"Never mind, Barkley," Kata says. "This is a good thing to do, sell apples on Columbus Day when everybody is out. I'm surprised you haven't done a spanking business here. Except that there're no walkers. Do you ever go over here to the marshes?"

"Yes, yes," the girl says excitedly. "Our dog, Wolf, he got lost over there and fell in the brook and was covered with mud and my mother wouldn't let him in the house and so we had to wash him with a hose and he didn't like it either."

"He is not accustomed to baths," the boy says.

Another car goes by and the boy calls out again.

"No luck," Kata says. "I'll take four more apples, though."

The girl takes a little cardboard toy box from under the table, opens it, and passes it over to her brother, who begins carefully counting out Kata and Barkley's change.

On a homemade ledger sheet the girl carefully notes the amounts received, change made, and profits. When the exchange is over, the boy inspects her accounting work.

"How much have you made?" Barkley asks.

"Quite a bit," the girl says. "Three dollars and forty cents all told."

"Actually, that is not a great amount, Jessie," the boy says carefully.

Another car, another lost customer.

"Maybe we should move on," Barkley says. "Maybe we're bad for business."

"It's possible," the boy says.

I can't imagine what he means, unless he is suspicious of the blue jay feathers in Kata's hair.

"Where are you going, though?" the girl asks when she sees us head for the woods.

"On our way to Concord," Barkley calls.

The boy watches us walk north toward the woods and then stands up.

"That's not the way," he calls. "That way you just go nowhere. You have to follow this road south for one and one half miles and then you'll come to West Street. You follow that and you'll see Pope Road on the right, but don't take it, actually, just go straight, you'll get to Lowell Road, and that will take you down to Concord, over the river. The well-known North Bridge will be over the hill to your left, which is east at that point in time."

Kata comes back to the road and looks southward in the direction he's indicating.

"Our idea is to walk to Concord through woods, without ever touching roads," she says.

"That's an impossibility," our guide says. "Roads are everywhere and you will not be able to cross that big brook over there."

"The one Wolf fell in," the girl says.

"Just what I fear," I say. "Do you know a way across?"

"No. It is not possible to cross without getting wet. You will have to get wet."

"Maybe there's a log," Kata says.

"Perhaps," says our guide.

"Well, we'll just give it a try," Kata says.

Just as we turn to leave, an old dachshund comes out from the drive, voices one perfunctory bark, and then stands at the edge of the road staring at us, wagging his tail.

"That's not, by any chance, Wolf?" Kata asks.

"Yes," the girl says. "He fell in the brook."

"His actual name is Wolfgang," the boy says. "His nickname is Wolf.

From: *Walking towards Walden,* 1995

The Iconic Dog

Setting: Dogs in world cultures

Dogs figure in some of the great voyages of mythology. Cerberus, the three-headed, dragon-tailed dog, guarded the gates to the Greek underworld. Aeneas fed him a sop to shut him up in the *Aeneid*. In Dante's *Inferno*, Virgil and Dante placated him by feeding him a handful of earth. Orpheus charmed him with a song when he descended into the underworld to retrieve Eurydice.

Mythical dogs weren't always bad, though. In the *Mahabharata*, the five Panadava brothers, including Arjuna and the queen, Draupadi, began their final pilgrimage to Indra's heaven at the end of their earthly lives. King Yudhishthira brought his dog along. At the Himalayas, all save the king sank slowly into the earth. Yudhishthira pressed on, trailed by the loyal dog. As he staggered, weakened, sorrowful, and blind with weariness, at the very heights of the mountain ranges thunder broke and Indra appeared in a chariot blazing with light and invited Yudhishthira to enter into the kingdom of heaven.

"Leave the dog behind," Indra commanded, when the king attempted to mount the chariot with his companion. "Dogs cannot enter heaven." The king dared to argue. "I cannot abandon the dog who has followed me all this way." The two of them were arguing in this manner over the meaning of earthly attachments, when suddenly, in a flash of lighting, amidst choral voices, the dog vanished. In his place stood the shining god Dharma. Indra praised Yudhishthira for his faithfulness and welcomed him to heaven.

From: *Walking Towards Walden,* 1995

Five Dog Night

Setting: East Charleton, Vermont, 1982

Richard Porter of East Charleston, Vermont, age seventy-nine, does not own an electric blanket. He does not have central heat in his three-room cabin, has not heard of modern airtight wood stoves, does not own a kerosene or gas space heater, and regularly allows the fire in his box-type wood stove to burn itself out each night around eleven o'clock. He is not averse to cold drafts and for this reason has never insulated the pine board walls of his cabin even though the temperatures in East Charleston commonly dip below zero degrees Fahrenheit for weeks at a time. And yet, in spite of his apparent lack of conveniences, Porter says he is never cold at night. He has devised a system of living blankets that automatically pile themselves on his bed in response to the temperature.

Porter is the type of mildly eccentric individual who can be found living beyond the confines of the rural towns throughout most of North America. He lives by his wits, working for logging crews whenever he needs money, picking over the local dump for resources he feels need recycling, and getting through the New England winter with as little expenditure of money and energy as possible. Like many who have deserted human society, Porter keeps a number of dogs for companions. Townspeople regularly see him walking along back roads surrounded by his pack, a mixed crew of all sizes and shapes, some large, some small, some friendly, and the rest too lazy to be unfriendly. Because of his companions he has earned for himself the title "The Dog King" among the townspeople. Not surprisingly, it is his subjects who keep him warm at night.

Each winter night about the time the box stove begins to cool, the first of Porter's alternative heating systems—a black and tan hound named Spike—begins to stir from his spot beneath the stove. Spike will climb onto Porter's bed when the room temperature reaches fifty degrees. Louise will get up around forty degrees. Any colder and the others begin to come in through a dog door that Porter has cut in one of his door panels.

Spike and Louise, his favorites, spend most of their time in the cabin. The others come in only to sleep, and only when it's cold. They come in a progression, Porter says. Jeff, a collie-like dog with a thick coat, will move in on those nights when the outside temperature reaches ten degrees and will join the others on the bed shortly thereafter. Alice, a medium-sized dog of indetermined parentage, arrives after the temperature dips below ten. But those nights when the mercury dips below zero mark the arrival of the warmest dog of all, an immense goldeneyed thing named Bull who has a strong shot of Irish wolfhound in his blood.

Porter says that Bull does not normally appreciate such bourgeois comforts as warm stoves and human companionship. But in his aloof, doglike way, he is as devoted to Porter as any dog of his type could be. Porter believes that it is generally below Bull to come in at night, let alone climb up on the bed with the lesser beings in the pack. But zero-degree nights get the better of his pride and invariably he deserts his usual hideout beneath the porch stairs and squeezes in through the narrow door panel. With Bull on the bed, there is not a night that Porter cannot endure.

Richard Porter has fallen behind the times in some areas of study. He believes, for example, that J. Edgar Hoover would have made a good president, is convinced that the Reagan administration is rife with communists, and was not aware of the fact that this country experienced what was once termed an "energy crisis." On the other hand, he has not been cold at night for sixty-five years in spite of the fact that he lives in one of the coldest regions in New England and spends no more than one or two hundred dollars a year on energy— mostly for dog food.

From: *Yankee Magazine*

The Cruelest Month

Setting: Scratch Flat

One mile from my house there is a field that once served as a horse pasture. Every year in April, usually about the tenth of the month, meadowlarks used to appear in that field and begin staking out their territory. I would hear them singing their plaintive whistle every time I'd walk by, and the song became a sort of signal, one of many in these parts, that spring was upon us, and all was right with the world.

Two years ago in April, as I was passing that field, I saw a backhoe parked by the side of the road.

I have come to dread the month of April. The officials who rule this community have decreed that any testing to determine the suitability of developable land must be run between the end of March and the beginning of May, when the groundwater levels are generally at their highest. It is not a bad rule, but it has meant that April has become a season of apprehension for those of us in this town who care about the fate of the earth.

The meadowlarks that turn up in the field each spring are not long-distance migrants. They appear from parts south just about the time that the forsythia blooms and the grass on the nearby lawns is turning green. The males announce their presence at dawn, and, if you walk by at any time of day and know what to look for, you can see or hear them. They choose a particular rock in the center of the field to broadcast from. Two weeks later, at the beginning of May, you begin to see the females, and for the rest of the season, as the grass grows longer and spring rolls into summer, you can hear them singing. By late May or June, when the nestlings are hatched in their little covered-over ground nests, the birds quiet down. But, if you watch, you can still see them, sailing past on their kitelike triangular wings.

Later in the week back in that fateful April two years ago, the backhoe moved out into the field and dug a series of trenches. A little later in the day, men with clipboards appeared and stared down into the holes, and that evening, when I went by, the trenches had been refilled. The meadowlarks showed up on schedule a week or so later and set up their territory. But I knew the meaning of the trenches; they were test holes, and the meadowlarks' fate would be decided by engineers with calculators in sad little offices decorated with calendars showing scenes of New England past.

Meadowlarks require open grassy fields and pastures for their nest sites. If the grass is too short, as on a golf course or a lawn, they cannot construct their domed, ovenlike nests. If the field grows too old and sprouts long grasses, young trees, or shrubs, they will not nest. And of course, if the field becomes a development, they will not nest. Common logic holds that they will go somewhere else. But current economies have dictated that there is no somewhere else.

In early autumn, after the backhoe appeared in the meadowlarks' pasture, a bulldozer cut a hole in the wall surrounding the meadow and drove what looked like a road directly into the middle of the field and then disappeared. The field languished in a sort of undeveloped limbo. Then one day the bulldozer reappeared, pushed some more earth around, and a few days later a sign went up announcing a new housing development.

By November more soil had been pushed around. By December foundation holes were dug, and the place that had been a field had evolved into a sort of strip mine, with great spoil piles of soil mounded here and there, bulldozers lurking at the former field edges, a few foundations, and of course mud, a veritable sea of mud.

By January the mud froze and was covered with a blanket of snow. By late March the snow had melted and the mud returned, and on April tenth I heard again the song of meadowlarks in the air. The meadowlark whistle is a sorrowful little song, repeated over and over. In better times it brings up deep-seated, pleasant associations—greening pastures, flowering crabs, the smell of soil, and a high, windy blue in the air. But last April it sounded what it is, rueful, plaintive, and sad.

North of us in the boreal forest where the majority of passerine birds nest, vast sections of land are clear-cut for pulp to make paper. South of us, in Central and South America, vast sections of forest are cleared for cattle ranches. Here in Massachusetts, in this indeterminate land of mixed hardwoods, suburbs, and fields, there is no such drama; the world declines in bits and pieces.

From: *Sanctuary*

Swanless in Pamlico

Setting: Wildlife Sanctuaries from Delaware to the Everglades.

Once in late autumn years ago, when I had more time and less money, my wife and I spent a month or so drifting south with the waterfowl looking for the big flocks that gather in the bays and sounds of the Southeast. We packed an assortment of camping gear in our car, (a nearly extinct Ford Falcon that broke down only once during the entire 2,500- mile trip), headed for the Gulf Coast, and eventually ended up on the tip of Florida in the Everglades National Park.

The idea of the trip was to visit the waterfowl refuges of the East to experience the huge congregations of birds that I had been reading about in other people's journals. These writings, which included everything from Catesby, Audubon, and the jottings of my birdwatching father-in-law, spoke of immense massings of ducks, geese, and swans—huge rafts of life and flights so vast they would darken the watery autumn sun. Never mind that most of these accounts had been set down long ago, before the world was turned upside down; we reasoned that we would see at least a remnant of the great flocks. Furthermore, we knew exactly where to go. We carried with us, as our Baedeker and bible, Pettingill's *A Guide to Bird Finding East of the Mississippi*, a text that spoke eloquently about hordes of snow geese and swans.

We began in the unlikely state of New Jersey at the Brigantine National Wildlife Refuge where we saw none of the congregations we were seeking because, as one manager told us, some fluky weather patterns had driven the geese southward. We pushed on for the mouth of the Susquehanna River where, we had been told, on a good day some 10,000 snow geese might be seen. There was a stiff chop when we arrived; the sky was overcast, a seamless pall, and the bay and horizon were empty. No snow geese. So we poked around up the river and at one point saw a bald eagle high over the water, headed upstream. As we watched, it turned and drifted south along the coast. We took it as a sign and followed.

There were a few good flocks at the Blackwater National Wildlife Refuge on the Eastern Shore, black ducks and distant rafts of American wigeon, but it was nothing to compare with the numbers we had read about. We met an old man there who was staring at the ducks through a telescope and shaking his head sadly.

"Once, in 1938, I saw a million ducks and geese out there," he said to no one in particular.

''Where are they now?" we asked, innocently.

"They don't come here anymore, " he said. "They're all down at Swanquarter and Pea Island on the Outer Banks. "

It was warmer on the Outer Banks. We camped in sad, windy, summer campgrounds, spent a night or two at the lodge at Mattamuskeet Lake where we understood we could see tens of thousands of whistling swans and other waterfowl. We drove around back roads, crossed winter-brown marshes, scanned bays and harbors and the Mattamuskeet Lake itself. We did see waterfowl, Canada geese mostly, a few flocks of ducks, and some swans, but these were paltry groupings, little island-like rafts in the distant blue of the bays. We asked an old man we met where all the waterfowl were.

"They don't come here," he said. "Not anymore. It's the corn; they all stay up on the Eastern Shore. Feed on the corn the farmers leave standing."

We nosed down to Hatteras, lost the muffler to the car, wired it back on, patched it, looked for birds, and drove back up the cape, swanless in Pamlico.

It was turning into a cold autumn. Sea winds chipped at us. We spent two nights in the car, drank thermos after thermos of hot black coffee and then, after another birdless search through the Cape Romain Wildlife Refuge, headed southwest for St. Marks Refuge on the Gulf of Mexico. We had met a man at Bull's Island. "Go to St. Marks," he said. "If you want to see water birds, go to St. Marks."

There was a stiff wind at St. Marks, spilling across the. marshes from Apalachee Bay and rattling the dry grasses ominously. We found an abandoned house with a crooked front porch and half-shuttered windows cracking in the wind. Hunters or reprobates of one sort or another had been there; empty shotgun shells, beer cans, and broken glass littered the front porch. Someone had broken in through a back door and started a fire on the kitchen floor. There were no ducks.

On the second day there we met a man who used to study birds in the Arctic and was friends with George Miksch Sutton, the man who illustrated our bible. We told him about our quest. He smiled a sad, St. Marks smile and began to tell us about flocks of shorebirds in the tundra. "If you're interested in seeing crowds of birds, you should go there sometime."

We went to Flamingo instead and on to the Everglades National Park. At any time of the day in the sky we could see spiraling gyres of wood storks or long lines of ibis. We watched them fly over Florida Bay to roost in the off-shore keys. These were not the birds we had been searching for, and we were told that even these flocks were sadly diminished compared to the numbers that were there in the 1950s, but seeing them against the sub-tropic sky, with a birdless continent behind us, we were almost happy.

From: *Trespassing*

Chasing the Chat

Setting: Martha's Vineyard

The yellow-breasted chat is described in various ornithological tomes and field guides as an infrequent and irregular visitor in Massachusetts. It is a catbird-sized creature with a yellow breast and a mockingbird-like song and, as far as habitat is concerned, favors catbrier thickets and patches of dense undergrowth. And although it is rarely actually seen in Massachusetts, it nests periodically from the Cape and the southern part of the state northwest to the Connecticut River valley, and sometimes even spends the winter here.

But where exactly does one find this elusive chat and how would one go about seeing it?

On an otherwise normal day back in 1995, I was drifting down the Nissitissit River in southern New Hampshire, not thinking of anything very much at all save the languorous beauties of a June day and the pleasures of the coming summer, when I heard a sad little warbling and mewing emanating from a brushy meadow on the left bank. I thought it was a mockingbird at first and then remembered a line from one of the many bird identification books describing the song of the furtive chat. I sat up abruptly and looked over my shoulder as the bird warbled on and the river carried me off.

Not to be outfoxed by mere downstream currents, I back paddled and steered the boat toward the shore, intending to land and find the singer. By that point the river had narrowed, the current increased, and before I could make the turn the bow was swept downstream again. No matter; I paddled hard on the port side to reach quieter water on the right bank to paddle upstream and try again. But in midriver the current increased once more and carried me toward a huge rock, festooned with deadly tree snags. More hard paddling, the canoe listing and almost shipping water, whereupon a small, energetic dog I had with me either fell overboard in his excitement or decided it was time for a swim and began a furious dog-paddle for the right bank, all the while sweeping downstream. I turned the boat again, skirted the rock with its armor of treacherous snags, made the shore on the right bank, retrieved the dog, and then carried on downstream.

But no chat.

That was in June. In July that same year, I was on the north shore of Martha's Vineyard walking along on the Rock Bight Trail, not thinking of chats, or much else for that matter. At one point the trail I was following broke out from the oak scrub and passed though an open glade of blueberry, thickets of catbrier, and low brush. There it was again, the sweet chattering and whistling.

I squinted into the thicket and moved toward the sound. Something fluttered in the thickets, and I stepped deeper into the greenwood tangle and waited. Silence. Only the sound of the field crickets and the dull thud of the waves down on the beach. The bird began to chatter again and I pursued more vigorously—much scratched by catbrier, poison ivy all around me, disease-bearing ticks abounding. Then I saw a shadowy form spirit off and drop down into a hollow well beyond a high impenetrable wall of catbrier.

No chat.

All this occurred at the end of a much longer quest.

Earlier, maybe even ten years earlier, in Old Lyme, Connecticut, not far from the riverbank home of the famous Roger Tory Peterson himself, my brother and I were walking toward the shore through an apparently deserted old field. At one point, I saw a yellowish bird rise up out of the brush, its legs suspended, and then drop down into the thickets again. Here I was in the very heartland of Lyme disease, barelegged and hot, ticks, mosquitoes, poison ivy, and catbrier everywhere.

Undeterred, I gave chase. Again to no avail, the bird had disappeared.

As I threaded my way back toward my brother, there came a hideous roaring and I saw a sweating baboon-like man with a red face and red bandanna headband just emerging from a battered jeep, already cursing my brother mightily and informing him in no uncertain terms that this was private property and that my brother and his type (not sure what his type was exactly) should get the hell out and stay off his private land or he would hold us until the police arrived. My thought was to hide in the thickets and let my brother take the fall. But the enraged landowner spotted me and started shouting again, pointing at me aggressively. I tried to assuage him with a stuttering nerdy explanation of my plight, that is to say, my lifelong desire to observe the elusive and rare bird called the yellow-breasted chat, a rara avis indeed, otherwise known, in the Linnaean system of nomenclature, as *Icteria virens*. This managed to disarm him briefly, and we were permitted to exit his property without a police escort.

But still no chat.

And so it went, year after year. A dog attack in Westport. Lost in the thickets of Chatham. A strange encounter with another offended landowner who actually took an interest in my quest and insisted on showing me all the improvements he was making to his newly acquired holdings (which in the eyes of an environmentalist were no improvements at all). And on one occasion, as I was emerging from reservoir land in southeastern Connecticut, a police interrogation. Why was I there on land that was clearly marked as off-limits? And my car illegally parked to boot? I explained that I was taking part in a national survey of a certain species of nesting bird known as the yellow-breasted chat. (Not exactly true, but mostly true; this was my own private survey and I had so far ranged from southern New Hampshire to Florida in my search.) This, I was informed, did not excuse me from walking on private holdings without written permission. Once again I was released with a mere warning.

And then finally, again, on the Nissitissit, one year ago. The same slow drift, the same meadow, the same warbling song, and, just before the current caught me, a yellow bird rose out of the brush, flitted off in a lilting flight, legs dangling in the style of chats, and dropped down again just before the river bore me away.

But was it in fact a chat? Such fleeting confirmation, so brief a showing, for so elusive a bird. Inadmissible evidence in any court of law.

From: *Sanctuary*

Why They Seek Light

Setting: Centerville, Maryland, 1950.

My father had a soft spot in his heart for fireflies.

We used to spend summers at a rambling nineteenth-century summer house known as the Reed's Creek place, which belonged to some member of my generally extended family. The house was set in a grove of cedars and was surrounded by hayfields, which rolled down to a wide creek where my family kept a number of small boats and a splintery swimming dock.

Often in evening, after sunset, my father would retire to the wide porch on the western side of the house and sit there, rocking and watching the hayfields fade from view. The first spark of light from the rising fireflies would inevitably inspire him to launch into some long firefly reminiscence, which his children, his family, and his visiting friends had no doubt heard before.

Part of my father's love of fireflies probably came from his interest in the Orient. He lived in China for three years and would regularly visit Japan during his vacations. While he was there, or perhaps even before he went out to the East, he began reading Lafcadio Hearn, the then-well-known essayist and interpreter of Asian culture.

Hearn was a folklorist, among other things, and something of a naturalist, and he had collected a number of essays on the rich insect folklore of Japan. Although my father grew up with hayfields and fireflies, I suspect that part of his appreciation for these insects came from his readings as well as his firsthand experience.

I don't remember much of the lore or reminiscences that my father would spin out on those long summer evenings, but there was one story in particular that stands out because it seemed to explain to me the logical way in which the world is put together. Periodically during those summers, in a Japanese folk tale probably lifted from Lafcadio Hearn, my father would recount the story of Princess Firefly.

It seems that centuries past, in the kingdom of the insects, the king of the fireflies and his queen had a beautifully bright daughter who came of age in spring. Her parents wanted her to marry, but she proved a fickle insect and in spite of the fact that a retinue of marvelous beetles, praying mantises, lacewings, moths, and butterflies came to court her, none met her fancy. As the years passed, her parents—and indeed the whole insect kingdom— grew more anxious. Each spring they would insist that she take a husband, and each spring she would reject the entire entourage. Finally, in order to please her parents and hold off the suitors, she announced that she would marry the insect who could match her own brilliant light.

One after another the brave suitors took up the challenge.

The great bronzed Junebug flew off into the darkness, seeking light. Hopeful moths fluttered through the night, lacewings and crane flies and even tiny gnats circled through the dark world hoping to steal fire to bring back to the glorious princess. In time the suitors found light in the tiny flickering oil lamps of country people. They clustered around the fire, circled it, or landed nearby and watched, waiting. Periodically one of them would dash into the flame to try to catch the fire, only to singe his wings and fall struggling to the base of the lamp. Try as they might, not one was ever able to bring back the fire, nor match the brilliance of Princess Firefly, and in a curious twist of traditional folklore, she never married and lived happily ever after as a virgin queen. But the poor suitors have never given up, and to this day they can be seen, flitting and circling in the dark night, battering themselves against lamps, ever hopeful after all these centuries.

There was always a silence after my father completed his tale. Beyond the porch, the river turned black. No one spoke. There was only the sound of the rockers on the old wood porch floor, the jug o'rum of the bullfrog chorus from the pond behind the main house, the quock of night-herons down on the dark riverbank, the sultry air, and below the house, like Japanese lanterns, the dancing of the lights of ten thousand fireflies.

From: *Stray Leaves,* yearbook of the
Massachusetts Audubon Society

Winds of the World

Setting: L'Île-Rousse, Corsica, 1962.

According to the Western Abenaki of New England, the winds of their world were generated by a giant eagle that lived on a craggy peak and flapped its wings continuously. Various nomadic tribes of central Asia had a comparable myth. They believed that the wind originated from a vast hole in a mountain somewhere to the west. And the Inuit of Alaska thought that the winds issued forth from an opening in the sky.

Here in the West, we believe that the wind is generated by the mother of all earthly things, our own star Sun. According to our legend, the sun beats down on the equatorial tropics, heating the air, which subsequently rises high into the stratosphere, creating a vacuum all along the equator. Because of a physical phenomenon known as the Coriolis effect, air from both the north and the south rushes in to fill the space, thereby creating, because of the rotation of the earth, the ever-reliable trade winds.

This basic system is much complicated by landforms such as deserts and mountain ranges, which churn and blend the moving airs, creating a variety of local winds.

Some of these, such as the foehn, are warm dry winds that flow down the lee side of mountains. Some, such as the sirocco, are bred in deserts and drawn northward by low-pressure areas. Many of these local winds are notorious for their strength as well as their effect on the human psyche, and most of them are named, a fact that has added to the rich tapestry of languages.

For a while, when I was younger, I lived in one of the epicenters of these local wind systems—the island of Corsica, which is tucked up in the northeastern corner of the Mediterranean and for this reason is subject to powerful winds from both the European continent and North Africa. It is probably not coincidental that the first place Odysseus fetched up after his sailors mistakenly released the four winds that set him on his twenty-year course of wanderings was likely Corsica.

Nine winds plague the island. In winter, the chilling mistral comes scything down the Rhône Valley, lifting tiles from roofs and screaming across the Gulf of Genoa to Corsica, where it is sometimes joined, or followed, by a companion wind called the tramontana, which blasts in off the cold plains of the Po. The sirocco charges up from the Sahara, carrying desert sands and hammering at the island as many as a hundred days a year. The grecale brings rain from the Apennines every winter. The levante storms in from the east. The ponente from the west. The mezzogiorno at midday and the terrana blows in at dusk, reaching its crescendo at midnight. And finally, there is the libecciu, the sickle of the northwest coast, where I lived. It crosses the Mediterranean and comes cutting in from Gibraltar, slamming itself against Cap Corse and beating the sea to a froth.

The winds of Corsica are an annoyance, but, except perhaps for the cold, bright, headache-inducing mistral, they do not seem to affect the islanders' frame of mind. Farther to the east, that is not the case. The meltemi, which is associated with bad tempers, screams out of the Balkans and strikes at the Isles of Greece. The traditional hot suffocating simoon breeds in the deserts of the Arabian Peninsula, carrying the dust and sand of the Sahara and causing shortness of breath and fretfulness; and to the west, in Niger, the dusty harmattan is believed to agitate local cattle. People in Austria and southern Germany say they can feel the onset of the mountain wind known as the foehn, which brings on a general lethargy, headaches, irritability, and may even be associated with thrombosis. And there is a northerly wind in Spain, the matacabras, that supposedly kills goats.

Here in North America, we do not lack our own ill winds. In southern California, the fire-breeding Santa Ana brings on asthma and hay fever and carries thick clouds of smoke and ash from its associated fires. In Texas, the clear sky-blue northers often signify an ominous change in the weather, and the famous warming wind of the eastern Rockies, known as the chinook, or snow eater, can melt a foot of snow in a matter of hours, bring on migraines, and may even have an effect on crime rates.

Fortunately, here in fickle-weathered New England, we only have two winds to fear—the rainy southeasters and the dreaded northeasters—which give rise to high winds and heavy rains, or snow or sleet or freezing rain, and sink ships, erode beaches, and bring on an internal chill that even tea and a warm fireplace cannot seem to banish.

From: *Sanctuary*

The Kingdom of Ice

Setting: Planet Earth

The orbit of the earth, as we were taught in seventh grade classes in physical science, takes the form of an ellipse. In one season of the year—winter—the earth is close to the sun, whereas, ironically, in summer, it is farther away. It is hot in summer, as we were taught, because the earth is tilted on its axis, so it gets a direct blast from the sun, whereas in winter it is tilted away at an angle and receives only oblique weakened light in the northern hemisphere.

But all are cycles—cycles within cycles as it turns out and because of these varying patterns of the earth's orbit there are periods, perhaps every 100,000 years or so, when the earth finds itself in a relationship with its parent sun that causes the whole planet to cool or warm considerably. This series of changes, known as Milankovitch cycles, has a dramatic effect on the seasons of earth over the ages, or so it is believed. During long stretches, the seasons are at extremes, with cold winters and very hot summers. Under these conditions, even though the snows build up each winter, the summers are hot enough to melt them away. But periodically the whole system cools down so that the winters are somewhat warmer and the summers are cool.

Whenever this happens—every 100,000 years or so according to the theory—the ice that builds up in winter does not melt away entirely in summer. As a result, a little more snow builds up the following summer. Then more snow the next year. And then after a few decades the snows fail to melt in summer, and soon the accumulated snows are so pressed down and so deep upon the solid earth beneath that they form a base of ice that begins to expand southward from the pole.

The reflectivity of the ice and snow feeds the loop, which makes the earth colder and colder. As these great walls of ice move, they crush the earth in their path, pick up seemingly immovable heavy boulders, ride over the very mountaintops, scour out river valleys, and press on, inexorably—a dreadful, deathly wall of ice, cut in tongues at the fringe but still moving ever southward and carrying with it its massive load of scraped earth and gravel and boulders.

The snows continue. The ice builds higher and higher, and deeper and deeper still, until the heft of ice is more than a mile thick in some sections and seemingly timeless in its advance; millennia upon millennia it presses southward Nothing can survive in this terrible season of chill; all life in the north exterminated, save for a few oddly situated pockets of protected uplands known as refugia. The whole north becomes a dead land, with only a narrow band of life crowded down into the sanctuary of the tropics and subtropics.

And then, as subtly as it began, the orbit of the earth alters once more, and the seasons begin to change.

About 18,000 years ago, the summers became warmer and managed, slowly, to melt away sections of the last glacier. Year after year, generation after generation, for thousands of years, the ice melted.

In spite of the hope and promise of better things to come, even this must have been a cataclysmic period in comparison with the deep overbearing silence of the frozen world: thunderous roars of calving walls of heavy ice, the great deep growl of roaring cataracts pouring over ice cliffs, streams and whole rivers gurgling beneath the ice like chattering voices, the crack of breaking ice sheets, the glassy shattering of pinnacles and peaks, and, all along the shores of the Atlantic, the incessant cannonades of heavy surf battering at the ice walls, with measureless mountain-sized icebergs breaking seaward in a surging wave to drift off and thaw in the warming seas to the south.

In the Northeast, where the glacier halted and drew back, it left behind its payload of sand and gravel, today's Long Island, Cape Cod, and the Islands. As it retreated, it deposited immense blocks of ice that melted down, leaving pools that are still with us today in the form of kettle hole ponds, one of which, Jamaica Pond, once served as the first reservoir in America. Within the icy body of the glacier, serpentine rivers, carrying loads of gravel, slowed and melted and left long winding ridges known as eskers—one of which snakes southward from the Mass Pike in Auburndale to the Riverside Station of the Boston subway system.

In some sections, deep holes developed in the ice, and within these holes were swirling waters, also carrying sand and gravel and small boulders, and these too settled to form small pyramid-like hills known as kames, some of which can be found west of the towns of Concord and Lincoln. And then finally, as the body of the glacier retreated, it left behind a series of whale-backed hills known as drumlins, of which there are many in the city of Boston and along the western side of the Boston Basin, one of the most distinct landforms of the region. Some of these drumlins were leveled for fill, but others remain as scattered islands that now lie in Boston's inner harbor.

The last glacial retreat ended around 12,000 years ago, and we are now in the midst of a new geologic age, a fast-paced one that is measured in decades and centuries as opposed to millennia. And for the first time in the history of the earth, what the shape of that new landscape will be depends not so much on orbital cycles as on the behavior of a bipedal primate that migrated out of the African savanna 200,000 years ago.

From: *Sanctuary*

The Slave Sale

Setting: The James River, 1830. Because of the faltering tobacco production, the owners of Greenwood Plantation are forced to sell some of their slaves. The five- year old boy, Marcus Aurelius (then known as Mac) and his mother, Lucilla, are among them. The owners of the plantation are fair with their slaves and are reluctant to sell them and break up families.

In August, 1832, rumors began spreading around his plantation that the master was preparing to sell a group of slaves. At this time in Virginia, the tobacco croplands were wearing out. In 1808, the United States government had outlawed the sale of transported Africans, although the trade still went on illegally. With the profits from tobacco declining in Virginia, and new cotton lands and sugar plantations opening up in the Deep South, there was only one profitable crop left, and that was the sale of slaves. And Virginian-born slaves were, so it was believed, the best trained, the healthiest, and the best workers.

As it turned out, the rumors of a pending sale were true, and one morning the overseer rounded up all of the seventy-five plantation slaves and he and the master circulated among them and selected ten men and eight women. Lucilla, Mac's mother, was among them.

Lucilla grabbed the boy's wrist and pulled him along by her side, half hiding him in her skirts. There was an old live oak behind the summer kitchen and the selected slaves were told to sit there in the shade and rest. About an hour later an angular man in a soiled linen suit and a slouch hat rode into the yard in a wagon, followed by three scruffy, armed white men on horseback. The three men were told to stay on the porch, while the man in the linen suit went into the house with the owner.

The morning stretched on. The men on the porch smoked. One came by and looked over the people seated under the oak. No one spoke. The other two wandered over and the three of them talked quietly, out of hearing. They kicked the dust, hitched up their pants; one of them spat. They pushed back their slouch hats. Smoked. Laughed at something, all the while glancing over at the collected slaves shaded under the live oak, some few looking back at the white men under their brows, surreptitiously.

The cicadas were whining in the fields. The heat increased and the people under the oak could see shimmering heat waves in the distant fields. Time was a heavy elephant, pressing on them. They knew, all of them, what was coming. Some of these people had been sold before. Some grew up on the plantation and were not familiar with the auction block. But everyone, young and old, men and women, knew what was about to happen. They lived day and night with the threat of sale and the break-up of families, mothers and fathers from children, couples, friends, and allies.

After a while the owner and the man in the linen suit came out and the overseer told everyone to get up and come over to the porch.

This was the dreaded hour.

Lucilla's hand tightened on the boy's wrist. What's happening, Mac wanted to know. ---Hush, she said --- But we going down the river Mama? ---he asked. ---- Hush up ---- she said. Her hand tightened. He scrunched down behind her back, hiding his face in her skirts, as if to banish the reality.

They stood in a line strung along the front of the house while the buyer walked up and down. He grabbed a young man's chin and turned his head left to right, drew back his lips and checked his teeth. Down the line, checking the condition of his future purchases, until he came to Lucilla.

Mac was hard pressed now against her back legs nearly invisible in her voluminous skirts.

"Do I see a little pickaninny hiding back there?" the buyer asked in a joking way.

He reached around and dragged the boy around to Lucilla's side. "What's your name little boy?" he asked

"His name be Mac and he's my only little boy," Lucilla answered.

The buyer turned to Lucilla and grabbed her chin, turning it from side to side, checked her teeth, felt her breasts and hips. She was tall, well fed, and full.

Good stock.

Of the eighteen people lined up, twelve were told to step forward. Lucilla was among them, and she pulled Mac out with her.

"He didn't say nothing about that little boy," the plantation overseer said to her.

"He's my only little boy," Lucilla said.

"We know that."

"Well I ain't going without him," Lucilla said. She looked over at old Massa, who was standing to the side, his thumbs tucked into his waistcoat. He looked away when she fixed his eyes. No words; she just looked. He was not a bad master as slaveholders go. Sundays off. Big, week-long Christmas holidays. Not a bad sort, and in fact reluctant to sell his people. But money was tight. Three bad years. He nodded back to Lucilla.

"It's all right," he said to the buyer, "Take the boy."

From: *The Sweet Revenge of Marcus Aurelius*, 2024

Rights of Salvage

Setting: The Concord River

Some years ago, I started a book about the rise of private property and the loss of common land, told via the stories of two disparate characters, Robin Hood and Henry Thoreau. Just as I was starting the book, I became involved in an incident that dealt with the same issue, only in my case, the conflict involved not land, but a canoe.

Not far downstream from what is now Mass Audubon's Brewster's Woods on the Concord River, there was an abandoned boat house, with three or four unused canoes lying around the building, overgrown with bittersweet and brambles.

In those years, I was on the hunt for a small, single-person, second-hand canoe, not a common item in the used boat world, and there, among the full-sized canoes, I found one. It had lain exposed to rain for so long that a mat of duckweed was growing on the waters inside the hull.

I used to walk that river trail over a period of years and all that time, the boat lay there, slowly returning to earth. At one point I heard that the property had been sold to a very rich man who had torn down the former house and built a mansion high on the hill above the river. Good, I thought, surely this new owner will rebuild the boathouse and salvage the old canoes. But no, the years passed, and the boathouse lay in ruins, with its surround of canoes.

Given this situation, a friend of mine, a Robin Hood sort of fellow, said I should just take the canoe. No one would even know. The real Robin Hood would, of course, agree. No harm in stealing from the rich to supply an impoverished writer with a cast-off boat.

But what would Henry say?

We know he believed that a man is rich in proportion to the number of things he can afford to let alone. On the other hand, he did own a boat (although he complained about the fact that he had to pay taxes on it). He also pointed out that money is not a necessary element of one's soul.

I grew up messing about in boats; they are part of my soul, so, according to Henry, I shouldn't have to pay anyone for the canoe. Furthermore, like his compatriot, Robin Hood, Henry had a little problem with the rich.

"The more money, the less virtue," he wrote.

Also this: "Lay not up for yourselves treasures upon earth where moths and rust doth corrupt and thieves will break in and steal."

If I, the thief, steal the boat, am I not just playing an existential role? The canoe in its current state is doomed. And anyway, when the tax collector comes around, the rich owner will not have to pay taxes on the canoe if I take it, so I am saving him money—not that he needs any more.

Given these opinions, it would seem that Henry would approve of the fact that I liberated the canoe and put it to good use, exploring the same waters that Henry himself enjoyed. Anyway, everyone has a devil in him that is capable of any crime, he believed.

According to federal law, it is of course illegal for me to steal the canoe. But then Henry's views of government are notoriously libertarian. It is possible that, in this case, I, an individual, may be right and the government and its laws wrong.

Robin Hood would agree, of course.

Ironically the owner turned out to be a generous sort and charged me all of twenty-five dollars.

From: *What Would Henry Do?* Vol. II, 2022

Saving Sherwood Forest

Setting: Englewood, New Jersey, 1952.

The year we fought the battle to save our Sherwood Forest, I was living successfully disguised to myself as Robin Hood. I was not the child of my kindly American parents, who had settled in the town two decades earlier, in the 1930s. I was, in fact, English, born in Locksley Hall, in Nottinghamshire, the child of Lord and Lady Locksley. My family estate had been undone by that villain, Guy of Gisborne, and I had eventually taken to the surrounding forest to live a free life of adventure and crime.

From the western windows of the castle fastness in which I lived before I took to the forest, I was able to see across the low valleys of Nottinghamshire to the Newstead Hills on the western horizon. From the eastern side, I could survey the veteran oaks and hollies of my adoptive parents' yard, and beyond, the rising grounds of the old brownstone estate wherein lived my nemesis, the evil Prioress of Kirklees, otherwise known as Mrs. Mackay, a woman who rarely saw the sun, dressed always in black Chinese silks, and periodically called upon the local sheriff's men to arrest me for my trespasses.

Beyond that property, past the grounds of William Parlin, Esq., through the boxwood hedges of Doctor Johnson's back garden, and across the meadows of Pitcairn Hill, lay the thickets and hollows of Sherwood Forest, a one-hundred-fifty-acre stand of ancient beeches, sweetgum, sourwood, oak, and maple where hawks nested and foxes dug their dens. This was no ordinary landscape, it was a haunted, overgrown tract with tangled underwood and massive trees. Decades before my parents moved to town, the nobles of a corrupted economic system—the robber barons—had built vast villas here on serried red cliffs above a wide gray river. The Depression had undone them, and they had lost their money and deserted the region for smaller dwellings in parts unknown. Wreckers, fire, storms, and other disasters had destroyed the buildings, leaving behind foundations, ruined gardens, pergolas, marble steps to nowhere, and broken-tiled swimming pools where frogs lurked in the remnant muddy waters.

All this combined to offer free range for generations of children who, in the less-restricted 1950s, were turned out in the morning to make their way, and were expected to return by dusk, in time for dinner and a warm bath. It is little wonder that in the wilds of this untrammeled environment we children banded together and formed gangs, and less surprising still that we should select as our role model the ultimate symbol of forest freedom, Robin Hood.

So it was in this guise, on a Saturday morning in September of that fateful year, that I set out from Locksley Hall with my loyal companion, Lord Barkley, a scruffy Irish terrier who was as fond of escapades as his master. The two of us made our way across the street and headed east, up through holes in privet hedges and across uncut backyards and woodlots to a small English-style cottage fronted by a huge magnolia tree. I went around to the back of the house and whistled under an open window, and a mop-haired girl appeared and said she'd be right out.

This was Maid Marian, my partner in crime in those years. She was not the demure lady of Angevin legend; she was small but fierce, had perennially un-combed blond hair, and could throw a stone farther and more accurately than any of the bad boys in Robin Hood's band. I suspect she had aspirations to be a girl Robin Hood.

There was nothing out of the ordinary in the adventure we were about to undertake; it was a day like any other in those years. The great dark boles and leafed branches of the veteran oaks of the old yards cast patterned shadows across the shorn lawns; the American robins were singing, the mourning doves were cooing, and the air was redolent with the odor of fallen leaves and cut grass, and we three—dog, boy, and girl—were living in that bright age when all the world was green and fresh and worth finding out about.

Maid Marian fled the house, slamming the screen door behind her, and we set out. Since it was still early morning, we cleared priory grounds without arousing the ire of the groundskeeper, a cruel Scot named Mr. McKenna, pawn to the Prioress and more to be feared than the local police, as far as I was concerned. He would sometimes hold me prisoner in his potting shed while he summoned my mother to administer the proper punishment.

Having successfully traversed this forbidden landscape, we crossed the broad lawns held by the Parlin family and burrowed through a hole in an overgrown privet hedge. From here we followed a narrow trail that skirted the gardens of the Templeton estate and passed in back of a ruined carriage house where we sometimes replayed famous battles of the Robin Hood era. We then crossed an overgrown meadow, made our way among Doctor Johnson's maze of boxwoods, and finally arrived at Sherwood Forest.

It was here, at the edge of the wood, that we saw it: nailed into the trunk of an old oak, menacing and nearly incomprehensible to us, was a freshly posted NO TRESPASSING sign.

Symbols of this sort generally meant nothing to Robin and Marian; we ignored them at will and carried on through whatever forbidden territory the signs were meant to protect.

But this particular announcement was different; this was a veritable offense against the rights of man.

It was a known fact—known, anyway, to anyone who knew us—that this woodland was Sherwood Forest. For generations, wandering troupes of local children had maintained their hideouts and camps in the hollows and along the stream banks. Here Robin Hood and his merry pranksters hunted the deer and the boar. Here they kept their fortress sanctuary in a hollow surrounded by immense boulders. Here they fought against the bands of sheriff's men who periodically launched attacks from the valley below. The tract was common land, open to all. To even presume to declare the area off-limits was unthinkable.

Soon enough the rest of our band of forest outlaws began to arrive. First to come was a skinny devil named Will Scarlet, a local troublemaker whose father and mother were respected doctors in the town. A few more of us straggled in, then the tall twelve-year-old named Little John, and finally Friar Tuck shambled in, an overweight ten-year-old who had enthusiastically assumed his role—he had even carved a special quarterstaff for himself, marked with magic symbols, in order to fend off the sheriff's men.

We stood eyeing the dread NO TRESPASSING sign. And then, without waiting for debate, Maid Marian struck. She leaped up and hooked her fingers over the top of the metal and carried it down with her. We attacked it and kicked it into the mud, pounced on it, bent it over and stamped on it.

Following this act of justified property damage, we skirted the western edge of the tract and soon enough came to another sign. This too we destroyed.

And then another, and another after that. Then, on the southeast side of the wood, at a pull-off at the edge of Walnut Street, we came to the origin of the offense. A massive sign announced in huge letters that this common forest was to be the future home of PARLIN'S HILL ESTATES.

The sign was mounted on heavy wooden posts, far too large to destroy, especially on a bright September morning in full view of the road. We retreated into the safety of the forest, where we began to spot surveyors' ribbons and stakes. These we snatched up and threw aside, until Will Scarlet, who had a passing interest in science, pointed out that if we moved the stakes by a few yards, rather than tossing them, it would slow things down even further.

We spent the rest of that day ranging all through Sherwood Forest, attacking the statements of the surveyors, and, as usual, replaying the adventures of Robin Hood and pausing only for a quick repast at Maid Marian's house, until finally, toward dusk, we disbanded. Marian, Lord Barkley, and I split off and headed toward our neighborhood. As we approached her house, we were confronted with an ominous (and familiar) sight: a police cruiser idling near the front door. We ducked back into the brush and made a wide circuit through backyards, privet hedges, and wooded lots, headed for my house and the safety of the hideouts I had created around my territory. But we were too late. Crossing one of the streets, the cruiser reappeared again and cornered us.

Two officers emerged. One was a heavyset younger man with watery blue eyes who seemed ready to administer punishment without benefit of trial. The other, an older man, was indifferent, possibly even amused.

Were we up at the Parlin tract this morning, they wanted to know.

No, we weren't, we said.

"You were seen there," said the younger interrogator.

"That wasn't us," Maid Marian said.

"Who was it then?"

"We don't know," Maid Marian said. "Bad kids from downtown. They always wreck stuff."

"Who said anybody wrecked anything?" the older officer said.

We were trapped.

"Is your name Linda?" he asked.

"Maybe. Who wants to know?"

"Well, Linda, you and your boyfriend here are coming with us."

Robin Hood and his merry band had been captured on several occasions by the police. We considered it an integral part of the life of a respectable outlaw. After all, Robin was often taken prisoner by the sheriff's men and later rescued. This time it was the usual procedure: we were escorted to the station, made to sit on hard benches, questioned, made to sit longer, until finally a parent was called to retrieve us. After a couple of hours, Linda's father appeared.

I was glad to see him. Unlike my own parents, he had a spirit of adventure, and although he didn't say so, I sensed that he was amused by our act. My parents, having had to endure the similar crises and crimes perpetrated by my two older brothers, were less tolerant. I remember waiting at the station on one occasion, having been captured for some offense, while the arresting officer called my mother, explaining that they had me in custody again. He hung up. Then he winked at me. "She says just keep him. She's not coming for you this time."

The fact is, however, our adventure that day in Sherwood Forest engendered certain legal consequences. Our argument, in essence, was that we did not know this was private property and felt that it was our land as much as anyone else's, so we had thought it only proper to make some sort of statement on the matter.

Living adjacent to our Sherwood Forest was a local naturalist, one of the few adults we would ever encounter in the depths of the tract. He had heard about our case, and he must have discussed the matter with a few sympathetic locals, who, I imagine, were no more interested in seeing a huge, ugly housing development appear in the neighborhood than we were. One thing led to another, and so began another battle in the age-old land-use wars.

A committee was formed to see what could be done to protect the land from development. The legal struggle that ensued carried on over the course of that winter and spring and involved many public hearings, a few of which members of our band and I attended. The long and tedious meetings, in which terms such as "fee simple" and "due diligence" were bandied about, plodded onward. From the hard meeting-room benches I daydreamed about Robin Hood and the ease of our guerrilla actions, so much more satisfying than this interminable legal banter. But in the end, the land was saved and was officially opened to the public.

At the time, I had no idea that our illegal actions to protect what we considered common land, and the features of the court case that followed, had been familiar events ever since the rise of the first human settlements and the creation of a land-controlling ruling class. Nor did I understand that our hero, the legendary Robin Hood, was among the first in a long line of land-reform activists who fought to preserve common lands for the people. He had fought the king and his minions in order to keep Sherwood Forest open to all-peasants and nobles alike. In his time, common lands had been seized by the king and declared out of bounds for all but his knights and hunting parties, by a series of acts known as the Forest Laws. Robin Hood and others like him actively (and, in his case, violently) resisted the king's edicts.

Over the next year, I quit recreating Robin Hood battles in Sherwood Forest and started going there simply to explore the nature of the place. But the earlier lesson about the value of resistance took. When I was twelve, someone in the town bought an old tea room that had an ancient copper beech in front of it. In order to announce the presence of his new furniture store, the owner cut down the beech tree to make room for a huge billboard.

I was outraged. (Robin Hood, readers may remember, loved to shelter under beech trees.) I wrote a letter to the local paper, attacking the criminal. And—probably because I was only twelve—they published it. After that, also because I was twelve, the letter was cited in other efforts to protect the environment of my hometown. It even garnered the approval of my long-suffering parents.

One line from the letter was repeated so often that I remember the wording, although I did not fully appreciate its forthright nature at the time: "It took a hundred years for that tree to grow. Where will you be in a hundred years?"

From: *Ecotone*, 2014

Forgiven Trespasses

Setting: The New York Palisades

On any Saturday morning in May, the birdsong would come rolling in my bedroom from the surrounding hillside long before dawn. I'd be up by sunrise, roll my bicycle out of the garage, and be off for the wider world before the dew was dry on the grass. I was ten, and the backyards were large and brushy and worth finding out about.

There was once money in the town in which I grew up. But by my time all the old families had grown eccentric. Their formal gardens had declined into a weedy patchwork, and frogs and salamanders had taken over their brick-lined swimming pools. Above the town, along the cliffs above the river, the world was even wilder. Here, in the 1920s, well-heeled stockbrokers had constructed larger estates, most of which had been torn down or deserted after the Crash. In the six miles of woods that ran along the cliff, there was rich picking for the unrestrained youths who ranged in the lower sections. And here, on any given Saturday morning in warm weather, we, the nomadic warriors of our neighborhood, would ascend.

I remember the tract well, a moist mid-Atlantic forest of sweet gum and tulip with the whisperings of gnatcatchers around us, and cerulean warblers, and the lure of ruins. One place in particular held our fancy. The estate was gone, but the pool, with its pergolas and terraces and statuary, was still there. Here we recreated the battles of history. Robin Hood and his band lurked in the surrounding greenwood to sally out and attack King John and his retinue. Here were Indians; here we fought duels in the style of the three musketeers among the moss-strewn statues and the shallow, rain-filled pool. The place, even at this distance in time, looms as a metaphor, a half-remembered country where the true tyrants of our world—parents— held no sway.

There were other sites in town. The old carriage houses, long deserted, had excellent burying grounds in the soils beneath the rotting wood floors. Some had elaborate stairwells, narrow and worth fighting duels to defend. We found the bodies of rats and possums and raccoons in these old barns, and we sent the resident pigeons aloft in wild flurries. One building even had a barn owl, I was told, but this we avoided inasmuch as it was carefully guarded by someone's eccentric uncle.

The town had streams and stone bridges over roadways into which large drainage pipes emptied. We had read or seen the movie Les Misérables, with its famous sewer scenes, and these too we replayed periodically. We tunneled down grates, through narrow spots, and into larger conduits that fed to the bridges and the brooks. Once beneath one of these bridges, a companion was attacked by a vicious muskrat who lunged at his throat, teeth bared—so he claimed—but only managed to get a bite out of his thumb.

It was here, in this landscape, that we learned the art of survival. It was here that I came to understand territory. Children, evil children from other parts of town, would sometimes sally forth and invade our grounds, and so we recapitulated history and defended our land with sticks and showers of stones from one of the old barns where we maintained our Fortress America against the Nazis, the king's militia, marauding knights, pirates, renegade cowboys, bands of thirties-style gangsters, and those myriad imaginary enemies of all forms who would assault our ground.

We found nests, we caught frogs and put them into our mouths on a dare, we collected salamanders and put them in fish tanks to watch them grow, we pulled clumps of onion grass from the moist earth and showered one another, we scaled the peaked roofs of a large nearby church. We brought home to nurse poor pigeons and English sparrows, along with baby rabbits, moles, and mice the cats carried in. Oscar the crow, who my brother rescued and who lived with us for years, always fixed me with his glinty eye if I ever came near him when my brother was not around.

There were no boy scouts in this tribe. There were no after-school programs. Saturday-morning television held no attraction, and personal computers, to my eternal gratitude, had yet to be invented. We were bounded only by the wilderness of our own imaginations. But, there are times when, staring at the child-empty fields and woods around the town in which I now live, I wonder in what fields the children of this lost generation of wanderers play.

From: *Stray Leaves: Selected Essays of JHM*, 2015

The Solace of the Rose

Setting: Western Europe

For my part, all this messing about in the garden while the Earth burns is not an idle hobby of a landed country gentleman with enough money (which I do not have) to waste on roses and new trees. But the fact is, I see gardening as an act of defiance. As the American ecologist, Aldo Leopold said in so many words: a thing is right when it works to preserve the stability and integrity of nature; it is wrong when it does otherwise.

There is a metaphorical aspect to gardening. To plant a garden is a not only a statement of belief in a future; it is a counter- balance to the act of tearing down nature for profit. It is the opposite of war, an act of creation as opposed to destruction. Place a seed, even in a flower pot on a window sill high above the city streets, and you become part of the cycle of life. Like a squirrel planting oak trees with forgotten acorns you establish yourself in nature.

Gardening is a resistance to greed and the capitalistic mad dash world of getting and spending. It is also—and this is my main point—a means of finding peace of mind.

It has always been thus, I suppose. The Roman poet, Horace, fled the politics of Rome and retreated to his garden. The Chinese scroll painters and poets of the 9th century deserted civil life and fled to the rounded karst mountains of Quelin to lead quiet lives close to nature.

Voltaire fled to Ferney, outside Geneva, and planted a garden.

Vincent Van Gogh retreated to a garden in order to escape whatever demons were haunting him. In 1869, he was committed the Saint-Paul de Mausole psychiatric institution in Saint-Rémy de Provence. Here among the patterned gardens and allées of the institution he found solace and comfort, and was also inspired to create what are considered by critics his best paintings.

Henry Thoreau went to the woods to live deliberately and there grew green beans in a clearing beside Walden Pond.

I suppose in some ways I was replicating Henry Thoreau with my own garden. Thoreau wrote that he planted beans, but harvested metaphors. By planting a garden he claimed that he established a balance between wild nature and the civilized world of nature restructured. By hoeing and harvesting he fixed himself in two worlds— the wild, untamed wilderness he so loved and praised, and the organized constructed world of agricultural civilizations. He wrote that in order to preserve his health and spirits he felt it necessary to spend at least four hours a day sauntering through woods and fields to free himself from worldly engagements.

In his case, as in so many others involving gardens, including Van Gogh, it was also a balm for personal disaster. Henry's brother, John, with whom he was close, died of lockjaw the year before Henry moved to Walden. His two year experiment living with daily contact with nature offered a form of solace unavailable in the round of normal daily life that he experienced while living in the town.

Thoreau was not the only planter who saw metaphors in growing things. One afternoon in the spring of 1939, while Virginia Woolf and her husband, Leonard, were living at Monk's House in Bidwell, Leonard was out in his orchard planting irises when he heard Virginia calling from the sitting room window to tell him that Hitler was giving a speech on the radio.

"I shan't come in," Leonard shouted. He said the irises he was planting would be flowering long after Hitler was dead. And in fact twenty-one years after Hitler committed suicide, they were still blooming each spring.

Literary and diplomatic careers notwithstanding, Leonard Woolf was a serious gardener, and when he finally got some land of his own, he went at it obsessively, "I'm always losing him in the garden," Virginia wrote to a friend (my own wife says this about me, incidentally). Virginia herself experienced two brief periods of happiness in her troubled life, first in the flower gardens of her youth and then again in the gardens at Monk's House.

After Virginia's suicide, during a period of his life when, like Henry, he needed refuge and solace, Leonard carried on clipping his hedges, tending his fruit trees, and cultivating the six acres of land at Monk's House. He gardened to the end of his days and listed gardening as one of his life's pleasures in his autobiography.

Ironically, the social critic and novelist, George Orwell, said more or less the same thing. He cited gardening as one of his abiding interests. He also favored growing roses.

From: *The Garden at the End of Time,* 2025

Solace and the Art of Scything

Setting: Scratch Flat

It's seven o'clock in the morning on June ninth and birdsong and sun are all abroad in the land. I'm sitting on my porch, drinking coffee and eyeing the grasses in a sweep of greensward that runs from the front of my house down a slope to a little shady alcove of clipped hemlocks on the eastern side of the property. My intention today, if things go well, is to mow the grasses, wildflowers, and ground covers that make up the body of the plant material in this expanse of open space. In order to accomplish this task, I'll use a scythe, a tool that was perfected sometime in the twelfth century and whose basic structure has remained unchanged ever since.

Cutting this section of my grounds is not a major piece of work; I could probably cut the whole strip in fifteen minutes or so with a ride-on power mower. But I prefer to make a project of it and mow by hand, mainly so that I can enjoy the morning. And it's a beautiful day withal; the little pine warblers are stitching the trees together with their sewing machine song; the cardinals are whistling in the thickets on the south side of the property; the indigo buntings are singing; the dew is on the vine; and all's right with the world.

In point of fact, all's wrong with the world. Earlier that year, a huge international coalition of Christian armies had once again invaded the Levant and local forces had, as expected, risen up to defend themselves. There was fighting in the mountains to the east; fighter planes and howitzers shelled ancient villages where, over the centuries, the local people, of necessity, would cast their lots with whichever violent tribal warlord held sway. To the southwest, the deserts were burning; the rivers were fouled with the wastes of war, the great marshes at the confluence of the two great rivers east of the Fertile Crescent were drained, and the Madan, a generally nonviolent unaligned tribe of swamp dwellers, were either killed or evicted.

But all that is out there. Not here in the garden. Not this morning, at least.

And anyway, in the long run, what can those of us who attempt to live quiet lives without praise or blame possibly do about an international conflict undertaken by distant heads of states over questionable issues about which we have very little influence?

With this in mind, I shoulder my scythe and walk around to the top of the greensward and begin to cut.

It rained last night. The clovers and grasses are wet and heavy, and the sun is glinting in little sparkling lights on the leaves of the ajugas and violets—perfect conditions for scything. The scythe snatches low, and the grasses fall easily as I begin to mow along the first row. I can hear the swish of the blade, the chatter of the wrens, and the chuck of the local robins, and smell the rich odor of cut grass and pungent weeds.

Scything is notoriously hard work if you go at it with brute force, but easy, even pleasurable and contemplative work, if you take your time, and rest periodically to smell the earth and listen to the birds and the crickets.

This is the first cutting, which is always the smoothest and freshest. I take a few swipes and walk on, take another swing and another step, and move on, slowly sweeping and cutting, sweeping and cutting, and mowing eastward down the line, leaving a two- or three-foot swathe of fallen grasses in my wake. The moist scent of fresh herbage rises around me, the birds sing in apparent unison, and from the farm on the other side of the hill I can hear a dog barking lazily.

It's easy to forget that elsewhere things are falling apart—wars raging in the Middle East, wars in Sub-Saharan Africa, civil unrest in Middle Europe, crime in the streets at home, corruption in governments, vast gulfs between the rich and the poor, armed madmen loosed on the towns. It's all storm and chaos and noise.

But not here.

In his novella, *Candide,* Voltaire may have summed up the state in which I currently find myself. Having traveled the world with his various companions, and having seen all manner of disasters, including the deadly Lisbon earthquake and the local Inquisition, and having retreated finally to a small farm in Turkey, Candide announces that in the face of it all there's nothing to be done but cultivate your garden.

In some ways that was the original purpose of a cultivated ornamental garden.

It was a hedge against reality. The creators of the great Italian villa gardens of the Renaissance were well aware of this fact. Streets and alleyways were plague-ridden and squalid in those chaotic decades; footpads and highwaymen, and warring city-state armies rattled through the countryside and the clamor of war was in the air. Better to stay in the walled villa gardens, lounging by the wellhead among the quinces and the ilex hedges.

I learned to cut with a scythe shortly after I moved to this land. I had recently been in the Azores, in the interior of the island of São Miguel, and saw an old man cutting a smooth green lawn with a scythe. I knew that the traditional American yeoman used a scythe to cut hay and wheat. But I had never seen anybody mow a lawn with one. In my broken, schoolboy Portuguese, I fell into conversation with the old man and he let me try to mow. The trick, I learned, was to keep the blade very sharp and cut low and slow. Actually, I never did learn the real art. But I still like to pretend.

No more than twenty yards into my work that morning, in midswing, I saw something leap in an angled arc out of the jeweled grass tangle—a wood frog. This is a good garden for frogs. In the forest just northwest of the property, there are two vernal pools where wood frogs breed, and, since this is hardly a manicured, pesticide-laden, neatly mown piece of land, they take refuge here. I can understand this. I'm doing the same thing. Theirs is a dangerous world, so dangerous that-unlike my own species—they are approaching the endangered species list. They eschew shorn lawns, paved driveways, and parking lots, none of which they will find here. But their presence in the long grasses is actually a problem for me.

Scything is quiet work, save for the whisper of the cutting blade. Frogs, snakes, grasshoppers, crickets, toads, and spiders (and also on a couple of occasions baby bunnies) do not hear the approaching scyther. This creates a dilemma. If ever I mow this swathe with a power mower, which I do every couple of years just to make a fresh start, long before the machine comes their way, the local denizens flee to safety. I hate to confess that more than once I have speared a toad by this scything work. Even the memory is unpleasant, and sometimes gets me wondering whether I should just let the whole garden go wild and stop cutting and trimming and planting.

In fact, perhaps cutting and pruning could be considered by some ethicists as a form of plant cruelty. A clipped grass blade or tree branch is in some ways a brutal injury to the organism. Plants have evolved the ability to grow back, but would it not be better to let them grow freely as they would in wild nature? I actually posed this question once to a biologist with a decidedly ethical bent and she assured me that it's okay to cut grass; it will grow back with vigor. "It's what plants do," she said.

In any case, the fact is if I quit managing this land the whole place would be taken over by invasive plants in a matter of years. As it is there is a lot of diversity on my grounds. I did a rough survey of the plants and animals in this acre-and-a-half garden one year and counted well over 2,000 species, which, I was told by an ecologist, is probably a very conservative count.

No matter, whether wild or tamed, the modern world is dangerous for wildlife: speeding cars, unchecked development everywhere, pesticides, climate change. It's also dangerous for people. A few weeks ago, just about the time that the violets, ajugas, clovers, and Quaker ladies were abloom in the mead, a mad man with a shaved head and an AKA-40 wandered into a public event and started randomly shooting people. The police stopped him. But as if to finish the business, another disturbed individual began shooting up the streets in front of a mosque. More shootings, this time in

Texas. Police killed an unarmed man in Florida. There were riots. Somebody tried to break into the White House. A friend of mine got mugged not far from the Boston Common, and everywhere there was bedlam.

When I first came to this property, I started using the scythe to mow the blackberry brambles and rampant orchard grasses that grew just outside the backdoor of the farmhouse where I lived. It was all part of a little fantasy I was playing out at the time. The place was a wreck in those early years—an early nineteenth-century farmhouse with canted walls, a caved-in barn, a few old apple trees, poison ivy everywhere, and on a rise behind the house, where a former apple orchard once grew, a block of ominous white pines that seemed to absorb all surrounding light.

My idea was to fix the place up and grow things there. Restore the land in other words. But I wanted to do it in the old way. Hand-tools only. It took me years, but slowly, working with the scythe, a mattock, shovels, and rakes, I managed to clear enough land to create a semblance of a pseudo-Italianate garden, a landscape design I had come to appreciate over the years. By the time I finally finished, I was living in a different house on the property, a house based on the designs of the mid-nineteenth-century landscape architect and house designer Andrew Jackson Downing.

Downing was a member of a loosely organized group of gardeners and landscapers known as the Genteel Romantics who favored integrated pleasure grounds complete with woodland groves mixed with ornamental gardens, fruiting orchards, and waterworks. Essentially they were escapists. They were contemporaries of Thoreau, Emerson, and the Abolitionists, but they chose to pretend that nothing was wrong with the world. They loved nature, but they believed in living modulated orderly lives. They weren't radical, nor were they Transcendentalists; they sought only the peace of nature.

I appreciate their philosophy, but I'm not that good at pretending. I try though. Anyway, I'm not the only one who has tried to escape into the myth of the garden in order to survive in the face of the absurdity of war, the destruction of the environment, the violence of the streets, and all the other ills wrought by the successful primate species known as Cro-Magnon. The garden is indeed a sanctuary if you can willingly suspend disbelief while working there. It can even be a sacred place for those who believe in that sort of thing. I used to know an older gardener years ago, an irreligious man, who somewhat ironically given his religious nonbeliefs used to talk about "cathedral time," by which he meant the hours he spent in his garden.

Halfway down the line I've planted a little circular garden bed in the center of the swath with an ornate urn, planted with long-lived annuals—yet another Italianate flourish in this American garden, and also a good refuge for snowy tree crickets. Later in the summer, I can always hear them repeating their interminable birdlike chirps in this spot, a sultry languorous sound that always seems to me to speak of fecundity and primordial life. I believe it was Nathaniel Hawthorne who wrote somewhere that, if you could hear moonlight, it would sound like a snowy tree cricket.

As early as late April you can hear meadow crickets calling from the grassy thickets here, also field crickets, and then in late June the fireflies collect in the air above this section of the garden. After that, in August, the snowy tree crickets, and then the katydids begin calling from the surrounding treetops, and then the dragonflies arrive. All this is made possible by the fact that the scythe, in spite of my best efforts, does not leave behind a shorn lawn. Even after I've cut and raked up the grasses, the vegetation is high enough to shelter all these native species of insects. This section of the garden, and in fact all the open areas, is more like medieval mead, a mix of grasses, herbs, and forbs. From April to mid-November there is always a variety of color here because of the mix of plant material.

I sweep on, one swing, step, another swing, step, little by little the land is transformed.

In some ways I hate cutting down this mixed tangle of grasses and wildflowers. But the fact is, I know that if I let it go the grasses and flowering plants will go to seed, turn brown, and lose their vitality. The crickets and the sparrows wouldn't care. In fact they would probably prosper on the seeds and the shelter. But I like the flowers and the new grown fresh greenery.

Out on the main road, about a quarter of a mile south of this property, I hear the wail of a siren, soon joined by the yelp of police cars. Something unfortunate has happened. Violence on the roads perhaps.

There's no visual disturbance here in the garden; I can't see anything but trees and greenery from this land. Noise is the only intruder. That and the daily news. I hate reading the news nowadays, but I do it anyway. Last week there was a major conflict in the ongoing desert war just east of the ancient city of Uruk. A big tank battle. Many casualties on both sides. This was not a good year for world peace.

Farther south, in sub-Saharan Africa, powerful tribes had clashed, citing ancient grievances. A victorious army clipped through the jungle terrain with the same ferocity as the warring armies in the north and east. Villages were attacked and burned, and an immense number of refugees fled eastward and southward, moving unseen through the vast Ituri Forest in central Africa, living on bush meat and thereby threatening the existence of local, and in some cases endangered, species of forest animals. The pursuing army cut a swath of destruction through the forest, driving the peaceful Mbuti Pygmies deeper and deeper into their forest sanctuary.

There is nothing new as far as the disasters of war are concerned. Save for a period of universal peace in northern India under the reign of King Ashoka around 323 BC, and a curious 100-year period of religious tolerance and general peace during the Caliphate of Córdoba in tenth-century Spain, the world has been characterized by violence.

If I have my histories right, the scythe as we know it was invented around the time of the First Crusade when a vast international force of Christian armies, encouraged by the religious fanatic Peter the Hermit, fought their way down through the Italian peninsula and on to Antioch, Byzantium, and the Near East and finally, after two years of warring, to Jerusalem. There were many subsequent Crusades, ten in all, and there were many wars in the region before that and many afterward, one of which was currently in progress on that June morning. Earlier in that month there was a pitched tank battle not far from the Via Maris, a place that archaeologists discovered a few years ago, evidence of what may have been the first organized war involving armies and sieges and the spread of empire—the city of Uruk, in this case.

We seem to have to live with this as a species. No one has yet beaten swords into ploughshares, even after generations of prophets and antiwar efforts and religions crying out for peace and love.

One day in the early years on this property, I was scything in the lower reaches of the mead nearer to the road when someone called up to me from the street.

"Cutting in the old way," he shouted, in a lilting Swedish accent.

I knew the voice; it was Sven, an acquaintance of mine who I used to chat up whenever I saw him walking by. Sven was a former gardener from Sweden. Even though he was in his eighties when I knew him, he used to hike the mile and a half to town and back. Sometimes on his return, he would take a shortcut and pass through the woods east of my house to collect firewood. I'd see him making his way up the road, carrying heavy logs on his shoulder for his stove. He was one of three or four old farmers who had been working the land in these parts since the 1920s, when a new wave of immigrant farmers replaced the original Yankee owners.

Sven and I chatted about scything for a while, how he and his father and brothers and cousins used to cut the meadows back in Sweden and how the adults would use the occasion to celebrate. They'd sing while they mowed and sometimes would hold a ring dance when the hay was in and get drunk and carry on late into the purple midsummer night.

Sven got me thinking about the famous scything scene from Anna Karenina in which the egalitarian conflicted estate owner, Levin, spends the day out in the fields with his peasants, trying to keep up with them as they cut the rows of wheat. He falls behind, totally fatigued, while they continue on with their slow rhythmic swings. But as he enters into the pace of the work, he slips into a state of unconsciousness, as if the scythe alone is doing the work. In short, he reaches that condition of timeless bliss offered by those who meditate regularly. He does not recognize the passage of hours until someone calls out to him that it is dinnertime.

It occurred to me later that I was a little like Levin, in an American sort of way (although hardly as rich). Scything calms the mind. The ambiance of nature obliterates the world beyond the moment; you live in the reality of the rhythmic work, the sweep of muscle, the unity of earth and air.

I grew up in an old suburb outside of New York City, and although I had farmers and watermen in my family of origin from the Eastern Shore of Maryland and had even milked a few cows in my time, I was essentially a city boy, not a countryman. Now, like Levin, I had retreated to the countryside to play the yeoman. I am sure my local farming confidants found me mildly amusing.

But never mind. All this is good for you. Recent peer-reviewed studies have determined that exposure to green space is salutary. So of course is exercise. So is meditation, and the therapy of certain aromas, as of fresh-cut grass, and even the presence of organic compounds known as phytoncides that are released by forest trees and shrubs. Also exposure to the sun—in spite of the possible danger of skin cancer. It's the best source of vitamin D, as well as regulating melatonin levels, which contribute to healthful sleep patterns and thus have a positive effect on mood.

I continue to mow eastward toward the shady hemlock arbor and the road, slowly cutting south to north, north to south, and back again, and all the while laying down the thatch of long grasses behind me. Whenever I stop to rest, I look back at my handiwork and notice that the tapestry of fallen grasses is alive with small insects, crawling, leaping, and burrowing back down into the tangle, their world temporarily upset, but unharmed. They will carry on; the grasses and flowers will grow back and life will go on. At least until winter.

At the garden bench in the hemlock alcove, I lean the scythe against a tree and sit down for a spell. I've made four circuits of this little patch so far, and there is a great oblong stand of uncut grass and clover in the middle of the space. Not much more to cut.

I give the scythe a few licks with the whetstone and then start down the island of remaining grasses, cutting and sweeping.

I asked old Sven once to show me how they cut hay back in the old country. He took up the scythe, went to the middle of the meadow, and began to cut from the inside out, making ever-widening concentric circles. Another old boy I knew, who used to cut salt hay with a scythe on the North River marshes when he was young, told me to cut from the outside in. Levin and his peasants, as I recall, worked down long rows, side by side in an angled line. In my little plot, I go along the edges first and work inward. I notice that later in the season, when the frogs and the snakes are out and about, they tend to move inward to the uncut swathe. So before I cut the final stand, I walk in and literally kick them out before I cut down their last refuge.

The sun is drifting across the forest canopy on the other side of the road at this point. The morning birdsong has diminished to a few errant calls from the catbirds and the ever-present house wrens. Summer is coming in; the mead is cut; and I'm getting hungry.

One more pass and I'll be done.

From: *The Garden at the End of Time*, 2025

Captain Maybe's Soliloquy

Setting; A bayou near Galveston, 1853. The former slave, Marcus Aurelius has managed to sell his master, and is now escaping with a privateer and his paramour aboard a top-sail schooner with a loyal crew of freed Africans.

By God, it's hot, ain't it, Queeny?" Captain Maybe said.

Queeny merely grunted and sniffed the marshy air.

"Reminds me of that time off Constantinople, when you and I were young," Maybe said.

Queeny huffed through her nose.

"What a heat, by God. Those were the days," the captain said.

"I wasn't with you in those days," Queeny said.

"Yes you were. You're forgetting."

"No, I was a little girl skipping on the wharfs of New Orleans back then."

One of their tiffs began and eventually Maybe relented.

"Well, anyway, those were fine times, they were, and I was young and salty and I thought I could sail on forever."

His talk, his mellifluous verbosity, began again and flowed on, rich with the sound of the dripping waters of raised anchors, the hum of wind in the shrouds, the cry of gulls, the sea mews, headland and harbor lights, and storm-tossed sailors home from the sea, blue skies with fresh fair-weather winds, and square-riggers hull down on distant horizons.

"God bless us all, Oh Lord," the captain sang out, "God bless those of us who go down to the sea in ships and on to distant ports, down the green tropic coasts of West Africa, the white line of surf and the boundless dark forest. And we sailed by for weeks, didn't we, on that first African cruise. It was as if the civilized world had declined into wild forest. Not a village, not so much as a thatched roof hut in view..."

"Give over, Captain Maybe," Queeny said tiredly.

"No I mean it, Queeny, you don't remember maybe. [Which of course she did remember, having heard his tales for a thousand and one nights.] I sailed the Mediterranean as a lad before the mast, Monsieur le Comte. I know those parts, those classic seas, the isles of Greece, the storied wine dark sea where every wave throbs with ancient memories, golden days and the shores swimming with amber and rose and aquamarine, and great skipping lines of porpoises. By God, if it weren't for family problems, I'd still be there now wouldn't I, back off the Corsican coast and outbound for Constantinople."

"What family problems would those be?" Marcus asked.

"Never mind that, my son, never you mind, that was long ago, and we sailed past Sardinia and down the Sicilian coast. I think it was there on that voyage we stopped to off load wine casks. Sailing out from Bordeaux we were—but never mind. It was a fine old time that was, before I sailed down to the Bight of Benin, and then over the open seas to Brazil."

"What was your cargo on the voyage?" Marcus asked, guessing that it was probably slaves.

Maybe dodged the question. "Coir and jute it was, and a rough crossing as I remember. Freakish headwinds all the way. September I think."

His stories carried on into the hot sub-tropic dusk. The becalmed schooner, its sails tightly furled aloft, lay still under a huge fire sky of setting sun and the night cry of herons and egrets sounding out from the obscured mangrove shores.

From: *The Sweet Revenge of Marcus Aurelius*, 2024

The Garden Wedding

Setting: Scratch Flat. Excerpted scenes from A Midsummer Night's Dream. *This book is framed by preparations for a garden wedding based on* A Midsummer Night's Dream.

The summer of the wedding proceeded day by day. The rains ended in late June and the heat rose, a slow, hot desiccation with day after day of sun, the scent of morning flowers, the air filled with darting hoverflies, dragonflies, and swallows, and still, hot afternoons when nothing moved. Heat lightning flickered in the western skies, and we could hear the rumble of thunder, but no rain appeared. Day after day with no rain. The peonies were long gone by then, the tomatoes ripened; the yarrow and the daisy, the hawkweeds, and the Queen Anne's lace bloomed, and by mid-July the fireflies appeared and the crickets began to call. And then suddenly, it seemed, it was late August, and the wedding day was upon us.

The actual day dawned with a merciful freshness, and out in the garden, life marched on as it would any other late-August day. The garden spider webs were jeweled with dew; the flies and bees buzzed in the hydrangea blossoms, the dragonflies awoke, dried their wings, and crisscrossed the open mead, alighting on flower heads to survey their next flight. The seed heads were ripening on the towering cosmos by this time, and goldfinches were riding the stems earthward as they landed and plucked the seeds.

By late afternoon the guests showed up in the garden in small leisurely groups. They helped themselves to drinks and wandered around the grounds, looking at trees and shrubs and chatting, until they were summoned to assemble in front of the Swan Cottage, where a cousin who had had himself ordained in some bizarre alternative religion, via the Internet, described to them the various "acts" of the wedding ceremony.

There was to be a traditional marriage procession in the style of ancient Greece, in which the wedding guests, who were provided with a variety of musical instruments, would march through the woods to a hemlock grove in Mr. Findlay's forest. Following the ceremony we were to exit in a recessional, led by the married couple.

The bride, a woman of original tastes, wore a silky antique wedding dress with tiered layers of eyelet she had purchased at a local thrift shop. She wore white gardenias in her hair, and she carried a bouquet of goldenrods, New England asters, and wood ferns. In order to be in contact with her Mother Earth, she went to the altar, such as it was, barefooted. The groom outfitted himself in his father's ill-fitting tuxedo, and he too marched barefooted to his nuptials.

They claimed to be a very religious couple, but they weren't sure which religion, nor which god was in charge, so they wrote a ceremony that included as many religions of the world as they could dig up, including some extinct, primitive customs. There were three "priests," one representing the ancient Sumerian goddess Inanna, and the self-ordained cousin, plus some sort of generic forest being who appeared spontaneously. We never saw the forest spirit's face inasmuch as he wore a beaked mask in the Venetian style, complete with the feathers of exotic birds. The couple had insisted that their resident dog accompany them to the altar, so we outfitted him with a Superman cape belonging to one of the children and adorned his collar with wildflowers.

The altar consisted of a table covered in white linen, with a stuffed barred owl, two silver goblets, two silver candelabras, and a teddy bear. The goblets and the candelabras were vaguely Christian, and the owl was associated with the goddess Athena. I never learned which religion the teddy bear was representing.

Led by a drummer, who sounded a slow, singular beat on an African djembe drum slung across his chest, we threaded our way along the woodland path, until we came to the place aforesaid by the master of ceremonies.

The bride was first married to a tree, a tradition adopted from one of the Indonesian island tribes.

The idea was that if things went wrong in the marriage, or if evil spirits attempted to enter into the couple's relationship, the tree would assume the hurt. The second marriage would be protected from evil.

For the tree marriage, the bride was tied to one of the ancient hemlocks with a silken ribbon. Then, as we watched, the forest monster leaped out into the clearing, and as if spotting us for the first time, glared around at the assembled guests, turning his head sharply from side to side and up and down, reviewing us gorilla fashion. Then, concluding that we were innocent, he said—in English—"This is good! I welcome you."

He then proceeded to cut the bride free from her tree husband, whereupon she fled into the forest density, followed by the dog in his Superman cape.

At this point the groom appeared, only to find that his bride-to-be had disappeared. All this was part of some other obscure, perhaps extinct, religion, and it was the forest being who saved the day. He produced from his black robe a bullroarer, a device used among the tribal people of New Guinea. It was a flat stick attached to a long string, which he wheeled energetically around his head. The stick spun on its thong and soon a loud humming began to fill the air. The sound seemed to be everywhere and nowhere at once. It was, we learned later, the very voice of the forest, and the trick worked. Slowly, the bride emerged from her hiding place behind a stone wall, and approached the altar, where the groom stood waiting.

The priestess Inanna was there too, wrapped in ceremonial robes created from curtains and tablecloths, with a tea cozy with a snake on top as headpiece.

At this point, words selected from various sacred texts, including those from extinct religions, were read. The bride and groom uttered vows in a variety of languages, and then Inanna married them with a traditional exchange of rings, in the Western style.

Then, led by the high-stepping forest spirit and the newlyweds, we danced out of the forest in a stately pavanne, accompanied by cymbals and tambourines, and the cacophonous blaring of toy horns and whistles, the dog prancing along with us.

The procession continued through the garden. We turned right in front of the Swan Cottage, and followed a garden path along the western wall, then made a turn around the circular bosque sacré and continued on to another circular path around a sundial, in the so-called Trellis Garden, then down the allée of the trellis, under the grape arbor and the clematis and the climbing nasturtiums, to the mead, where we then turned right again and entered the orchard. The happy throng passed through the gate of the hornbeam wall, turned left, and then left again in front of the teahouse, and danced down between the flower beds, to the Lady Garden, all bright in that season with the purples and reds and yellows and the blue carpet of creeping thyme. The horns still blaring and the cymbals and bells still jangling, the group turned right again and proceeded through a privet-lined path to the maze, which they entered and threaded through. At the goal, the very center of the labyrinth, which is traditionally the entrance to the underworld, the bride and groom halted and exchanged a second ceremonial kiss, which perhaps went on a little too long for such a seriously religious wedding as this.

From: *An Eden of Sorts*, 2019

PART FIVE:
DENOUMENT

Evensong

Setting: Scratch Flat. Last evening in a Thoreauvian cottage I lived in for a couple of years.

By June 21 I had been living in my cottage for one year. It rained that night, a warm, sustaining rain that dripped off the leaves in the hickory grove and filtered down through the tangle of wildflowers into the soil of the meadow. Just before going to bed I went out and stood in the open air, allowing the cleansing coolness of the sky to fall over my shoulders. I was alone, and below the meadow, in my old house, a light was burning, a brighter reflection of the warmer light of the oil lamps in my cottage. I thought of a flicker I had heard the night before. For some unknown reason, in the middle of the night, it had let out a long whinny from the woods beside the cottage. The sound woke me instantly, and I felt a strange sense of communion with the bird—a fellow traveler in the experiment of life, a spark in a generally lifeless and desolate universe. I felt a similar communion seeing the light below the meadow. I felt that I and my family, my friends and allies and acquaintances, were all shrinking down into the small, wild spaces of the world. I was determined now to stay on.

The rain slowed, spilled to a mere drip in the surrounding woods; a cricket started up, and deep in the mat of grasses on the south side of the meadow I saw the bright flash of a firefly.

From: *Living at the End of Time*, 1990

Farewell to Fuji

From my father's China journals.
Setting: 1918, Leaving Yokohama, after three years
in Warlord China.

There is an emotional thrill in all leave-taking, and it is particularly keen when a big ship puts off. In our case too we were going home - most of us after years in the Orient.

And when one goes home in wartime, it is to unknown conditions and an unknown future.

The crowd on the ship cracked jokes and made light of it, as people always do when they really feel a thrill. They broke jokingly into "Over There" as we warped away from the dock, but they really meant it: "The Yanks are coming, the Yanks are coming; and we won't be back until it's over over there." There was cheering on the dock and the usual waving of hats and handkerchiefs.

A puffing tug pulled our bow around until we headed out between the red and white lighthouses which mark the breakwater of Yokohama harbor. And we steamed slowly out and into the blue-green water and whitecaps of the Pacific. It had been 96 degrees in the shade in Yokohama; out in the harbor there was a splendid cool breeze. The skyline was piled up with fleecy white clouds and so we could not see Fuji to say goodbye. We were sorry for that, for there is a superstition that unless one can say goodbye to Fuji as he leaves Yokohama harbor, he is not coming back to the East.

A Lament for the Great God Pan

Setting: the Italian peninsula

There is a Christian legend that deals with Pan. In some versions it takes place at the birth of Christ, in others it occurs on the day of the Crucifixion and the renting of the temple veil, but in any of these various forms it involves travelers, usually sailors. In one story, pilgrims are voyaging off the coast of Tuscany. In another they are approaching the Oracle at Delphi. And in another, one of the earliest, they are near the coast of southern Italy, becalmed off the island of Oaxi.

As the sailors approach the coast, the wind suddenly drops, the air thickens and an odd stillness hangs over the land and sea. All day the sailors wait, and then towards evening, a great thundering voice rings out in the upper air and rolls across the nearby hills and vales declaiming the news:

"The Great God Pan is Dead."

Suddenly, from all the hills and streams, from the little hidden valleys, from temples and sacred groves, from mountain pastures and ferny cliffs and brakes, from bubbling brooks and spring banks, from every wild quarter of Italy there rises a great singular, tragic cry of lament, a vast outpouring of wailing and weeping and shrieking that echoes across the hills and valleys and spreads all across the Italian peninsula. Pan, Pan is dead.

After this event the Greek oracles no longer prophecy accurately. The old gods of the Peninsula, the genies of all the old sacred places, the Dianas of the Wood, the nymphs of all wild nooks, the dryads and hamadryads of the trees, the oreads of caves and grottoes, the naiads of the lakes and streams, the fauns and satyrs and centaurs, and all the wild things, fall silent and retreat. The Lord of the Wood is dead, the ancient god of the wild, and the world now has in his place a new king whose domain is not earth but heaven.

There has been much analysis of this alleged event and the story has been altered by folklore and legend so that the locale has changed and also to some extent the period in which the event took place. But as is often the case with myth, the folklore is a reflection of history. The old order was indeed dying, and the new, heaven-in-spired, mystic religion of the followers of Christ was near at hand.

John Milton sums up this moment in his poem "Hymn on the Morning of Christ's Nativity" with a description of the shepherds in their pastures thinking on mighty Pan, followed by the forlorn silence of the oracles after Christ's birth. Milton describes the hollow prophecies of Delphos, the lonely, god-deserted mountains, the sound of weeping and lamenting from all the haunted springs and dales. All the storied spirits of these sacred spots retreat with a sigh—flower-tressed nymphs with flowing hair mourn in the tangled thickets, the ancient, powerful gods of the pre-Hellenic tradition—Astarte and Tamuz, Isis, Horus, and Anubis—begin lamenting with a drear and dying sound. Wild nature and its minions and all its gods, demi gods, nymphs, satyrs, and centaurs, retreat, sorrowing, in the face of the coming of the true God.

"Pan, Pan is dead, the Great God Pan is dead," is a phrase that was picked up and used later by poets and playwrights. And it is probably true that the classical world of which Pan was so much a part, the old images that appear again and again in the niches and rooms of Italian gardens, and in fact the whole metaphor of the Italian gardens themselves, with all their underpinning of mythology and history may be lost. You wander around the museums, public parks and gardens of Europe and you see the graven images of all these forgotten gods and heroes, old Pan and Procreus, Artemis and Titan and Neptune, and half the tourists you encounter, probably more, don't know who is chasing whom and who got turned into a tree by whom having been chased by which god. I include myself in this group, even though I grew up with these stories—my mother having instilled them in me since ever I was able to understand.

But throughout it all Pan was never really lost. The ancient Lord of the Wood is everywhere in the modern world, even if he has to take the image of the devil himself. And anyway, the real Pan, the spirit of Pan, the spirit of the wild, has never been so alive. Thoreau knew all about him and his fellow gods and demigods. He didn't dare venture any farther up Katahdin because of the overbearing presence of the Olympian Gods. Emerson found Pan in Italy and brought him home to America, so did Hawthorne, so did Cole, and Church and John Muir. Rachel Carson knew about Pan, so did Edward Abbey and old Paul Brooks and all the other twentieth century advocates of wilderness and wild nature. The soul of Pan, his energetic, fecund spirit, was effectively reborn in the as yet unspoiled open reaches of nineteenth century America, those wilderness temples of John Muir and company.

Pan is very much with us. And it is not necessary to outfit expeditions into the remnant wilderness at the uttermost ends of the earth in order to find him. Just go out to some nearby dark wood on a moonless night, bushwhack thirty yards into the thickets without a flashlight, stand still for a few minutes and wait.

He'll be there.

From: *The Wildest Place on Earth*

Leaving la Belle Isle

Setting: Leaving L'Île-Rousse Harbor, Corsica

A few nights later, after dinner, Jean-Pierre poured me a glass and sat with me out on the terrace.

"It looks like the season is over," he said. "It is finished. And so for you…" He spread his palms with a helpless shrug.

"I know," I said. "I have to get back anyway."

"The *Bagheera* is coming in a couple of days.; I can arrange passage for you to Marseille," he said.

We drank quietly, watching the harbor and the causeway, as one by one the card players began to arrive: Max first, then Jacqui, then André. They greeted us, shaking hands all around, lazily, and went over to their table on the harbor side of the terrace and sat staring out at the harbor. Waiting. After a while, Jean-Pierre said he should probably join them. He rose, walked over and sat down, and accepted whatever hand was dealt to him.

I left with Chrétien a few days later. We stood on the quay with Vincenzo, Jean-Pierre, and Micheline, smoking and making small talk and watching the stevedores argue over the great nets of cargo that were lowered from the decks.

Jean-Pierre drew me aside to say goodbye and pressed a thick manila envelope into my hands.

"For you," he said. "For all the fish and dishes."

We shook hands all around and kissed and pounded one another's shoulders, and Lucretia buried me in her arms and sniffled. Then Chrétien and I boarded and stood in the stern as the old vessel rumbled and growled, made its turn, and headed out from L'Île-Rousse harbor.

The freighter rounded the jetty and laid a straight course northward, a few gulls following and a long stream of dancing furrows spreading astern in a north-facing arrow. The promenade along the shore grew smaller; the red-tiled roofs of the Rose Café receded, blended with the surrounding rocks, and then disappeared. Then the town diminished, leaving only the judgmental nuns hovering above. Then the nuns faded, and all I could see were the jagged, indifferent heights of the interior.

For a while, the island floated above the horizon, a gray wash of abstracted peaks, unattached to anything tangible in the midst of a turquoise sea. The engines thrummed below me with a rhythmic *thud*. I caught a whiff of the maquis, and as I watched, the ambiguous peaks slowly faded to memory—a rose-red island where blue-green valleys swept down to the sea, and sea rolled out to the wide azure sky.

From: *The Rose Café*

Descent of the Chariot of the Sun

Setting: Lewes Island, Outer Hebrides

On the evening of the solstice, after dinner, around eleven o'clock, I wandered out to the site again. Now I was not alone. Several people, some of them obviously local, some obviously strangers to this place, had come out and were sitting on the ground, facing west, watching the skies. There was a black cloud lying along the western horizon, like a dark, sleeping dragon, its slightly upturned pointed nose resting on the northern horizon line and its riffled, jagged back already glowing in gold. The sun was still above the cloud, and still to the south of the standing stones, and there was heated discussion as to whether it would be obscured in its descent by this dragon-cloud. From my point of view, it looked as if the sun would drop into the sea well to the south of the short avenue of stones, but I was assured that, as it sank, it would be sweeping northward along the sea and drop down near the avenue line.

One fellow in a tan windbreaker and a deerstalker cap was especially keen on celestial observations at this site and was setting up a quadrant.

He was intensely mathematical in his observations and had charts and graphs and record books of the rising dates of various stars from ancient times onward, and was calculating the solar angle and the like, checking his chronometer every minute or two and marking the time and the angles.

Others were not concerned with the science, but with the holiness of the place. One man wore a silver Celtic cross on a chain around his neck, and there was a small group in Druid hoods and robes, and two long-haired couples in beads and loose, Indian clothing sitting some distance off from the site, honoring the temple by smoking a sacred herb that they ritually passed among themselves with ceremonial formality.

As the sun drew nearer its descent, the collected few grew quieter, and then quieter still, and by the time the sun reached the horizon, they spoke only in whispers, if at all. I drew apart and moved back to the east slightly to get a good view of the whole scene—the temple, the people, the loch beyond, the small island lying just beyond the loch to the southwest, and of course the great blue arc of the sky, the black dragon-cloud, and this honored god, the sun, who imperceptibly moved along the line of the sea, as if unwilling to let go his handhold of day.

The great fiery horses of the solar orb, those who fed on the fields of ambrosia by night, could not be seen, nor could we see the golden, resplendent chariot of Helios. The sunhorse of Trundholm bog was not visible, nor the barge of Ra, nor the Vedic charioteers, nor Sula, nor Sol, nor Surya. But they must have all been there that evening, hard at work, slowly reining in the horses, steering the chariot of the sun ever downward at a decreasing angle into the western sea. Their work for the day was almost over.

Just to the north, as if in reaction to the sun's mighty presence, the dragon-cloud began raising his head and twisting himself into unlikely shapes, transforming himself, as dragons will, into various configurations. Now he was a tower, then he became a hill, and then, as if in surrender, he began to break apart, and moved upward to join the golden, fretted sky, which by now was charged with greens and reds and rays of blue and black in those places where the cloud had spread out.

And then, in a hushed silence, almost humbled, the great god sun, the source of all life on earth, dropped with his horses into the sea. First his light touched the sea rim, the ball of flame moved downward and distorted into an ellipse, and, as we watched, the ellipse spread out and became a glowing pool of gold.

A minute later it was gone.

From: "Following the Sun," 2002

Acknowledgements

The essays and excerpts in this book originally appeared in a variety of journals and books.

Many of the essays appeared first in *Sanctuary*, the journal of the Massachusetts Audubon Society published between 1980 and 2016. Early editions of the books were published by Houghton Mifflin, Perseus Books, and Counterpoint Press, as well as a number of smaller presses.

I had the help and support of a variety of editors and publishers, including the first editor of Mass Audubon publications, Wayne Hanley, a well-seasoned old newspaper man who hired me and taught me the art of the interview. After he retired, I took his place and, with the help of Jerry Bertrand, president of the Society, came up with the idea of publishing a journal called, *Sanctuary*, that focused on a single theme for each edition.

As far as the books are concerned—fourteen so far—I had the support of several different editors. First and foremost among these include Merloyd Lawrence, who from the start, until her death in 2022, encouraged my work and was the editor of six of the books from which the excerpts were taken. My earliest, and equally supportive editor, was Harry Foster of Houghton Mifflin, and later, Jack Shoemaker, the founder and editor of Counterpoint Press.

Other thanks include the host of writers who contributed to *Sanctuary* over the years, as well as the many readers and reviewers who have followed my work.

And, finally, thanks to the wide range of family members who watched over me all these years. My mother, of course, enjoyed my writing, so did my older brothers, James and Hugh, both of whom have walk-on parts in my books, although my oldest brother, James, took umbrage over my description of his eating habits that appeared in my early book *Living at the End of Time*:

"He feeds on bananas and peanut butter and the occasional chocolate donut."

I also enjoyed the loyality of my children Clayton and Lelia, and also my wife and copy-editor, Jill Brown, my stepsons Alexander and Gabriel, and my cousins from the Eastern Shore of Maryland.

Although he didn't live long enough to read anything I have written, I think my greatest influencer (and also critic) was the prose of my father, an Anglican minister of the old school who kept journals from his college years throughout his life including the journals of his three years in Warlord China, which, in 2018, my brother Hugh and I published as *Travels in a Vanishing Empire*. His journals, and some of his published magazine stories, are written with the easy fluency of so many of the writers of his era.

To wit: The first lines of his European journals written in the politically critical summer of 1937.

June 23rd, 1937 On board *Europa*
Tonight, at dusk, I first saw England.
I came out from dinner to the promenade deck—and there, suddenly, unexpectedly, was land—a solid hilly stretch on the near horizon, black against low-lying rosy clouds to the northwest. Out on the dark stretch of land was a bright, steady light, and along the coast, other lights winked on the hilltops. Years of travel in the Orient have made me overly blasé to new sights but, at the sight of England, the thrill of discovery came rushing back, overwhelmingly. I had never seen this rocky land before, but here was the dark shore of England, the place of years of study, the deep history, the ancestral lands. I felt like I was finally returning home.

John Hanson Mitchell is an American author with
a back list of sixteen books, six of which deal
with a square mile of agricultural land in Eastern
Massachusetts known as Scratch Flat. Mitchell has
used the tract to explore his continuing interest in
the interrelationship between nature and human
cultures throughout history. Other books deal with
travel, memoir, and his discovery of the first African
American landscape photographer Robert A Gilbert
(1869 -1941). He is also the author of two novels, one
of which (*The Sweet Revenge of Marcus Aurelius*) is
based on the true story of a slave who sold his master.

Mitchell was the editor (and founder)
of the environmental journal *Sanctuary*,
published by the Massachusetts Audubon
Society between 1983 and 2016.